# *Beyond the Code: Discove* ⦀⦀⦀
## *Intelligence*

I0012660

Index:

# Chapter 1: Fundamentals of Artificial Intelligence

## Definition

Artificial Intelligence, often abbreviated to AI, is an interdisciplinary field of study that seeks to simulate or replicate human intelligence in machines. This seemingly simple definition belies a remarkable depth and complexity, since intelligence itself is an elusive and multidimensional concept. So what does it mean to "simulate" or "replicate" intelligence? And what do we mean, more specifically, by intelligence?

Traditionally, intelligence has been viewed as the ability to acquire and apply knowledge and skills. However, in a broader context, it can also include other forms of problem solving, creativity, emotional adaptability, and even intuition. When we transfer this concept to the machine world, the definition becomes even more elusive. Unlike humans, machines have no biological consciousness, emotion, or instinct. So, to what extent can a machine be considered "intelligent"?

In the context of AI, intelligence is often understood as the ability of a machine to perform tasks that, if performed by a human, would require the application of intelligence. These tasks can range from simple data processing and calculations to complex problem solving, learning and adaptation to reasoning and planning.

One of the major hurdles in defining AI is its segmentation into various sub-disciplines and approaches.

Some areas of AI focus on specific problems, such as voice or image recognition. Others explore more general issues related to machine learning, logic, and optimization. There are also branches of AI that deal with human-machine interaction, trying to make machines more "understandable" and "natural" in the way they interact with humans.

Technology has reached a point where machines can not only perform specific tasks that require forms of intelligence, but also learn from data and experience, adapting to new situations. This marks a significant turning point: AI is no longer just a set of rules programmed into a machine, but a system capable of "learning" in a similar, though not identical, way to a human being.

Artificial intelligence is, therefore, a rapidly evolving field that continually challenges our pre-existing conceptions of what a machine can and cannot do. And as we move towards a future in which AI becomes increasingly integrated into our lives, it is crucial to understand what kind of "intelligence" we are actually building, and what its ethical, social and human implications will be.

With this definition as a starting point, we can now explore the various aspects of artificial intelligence in detail, trying to understand not only how it works, but also how it is transforming our world in ways that might have seemed inconceivable just a few years ago.

## Fundamental Features

Learning: Much of modern AI is based on machine learning, which allows systems to learn from data rather than being explicitly programmed.

This learning can occur through examples (supervised learning), experimentation (reinforcement learning), or identifying patterns in the data (unsupervised learning). This concept lies at the heart of modern AI. Machines learn from data and past experiences, adjusting their algorithms to improve performance over time.

Reasoning: AI can simulate human reasoning to solve specific problems, such as in symbolic AI or logic programming.

Self-correction: An AI system can review and correct its decisions based on new data or feedback.

Interaction: Many AI systems can interact with users or other systems in advanced ways, such as through natural language understanding or computer vision.

Automation: AI has the potential to automate repetitive and tedious tasks, freeing up human time for more creative and strategic pursuits.

Neural Networks: Inspired by the structure of the human brain, artificial neural networks are systems of algorithms that allow machines to recognize complex patterns in data. Deep neural networks are capable of learning increasingly abstract representations of data.

## Types of Artificial Intelligence

Narrow AI (or Narrow AI): This form of AI is designed and trained to perform a specific task without human awareness or emotional intelligence. Examples include virtual assistants like Siri or Alexa or image recognition programs.

General AI (or AGI, Artificial General Intelligence): This type of AI will have all the cognitive capabilities of a human, allowing it to perform any intellectual task that a human can do.

At present, AGI remains a theoretical target.

Superintelligent AI : Refers to a future in which the cognitive capacity of machines will far surpass that of humans in almost all fields.

# Historical evolution

## The Philosophical Origins

The philosophical origins of Artificial Intelligence (AI) go back a long way, well before the era of modern computing and engineering. The philosophical roots of AI can be traced back to ancient thinkers who questioned the relationship between mind, consciousness and matter.

Aristotle, one of the greatest philosophers of antiquity, developed the concept of "rational soul" as a principle that gave form and function to the human body. His ideas about logic were eventually codified into a form that laid the foundation for computer rule programming, one of the central aspects of symbolic AI. The Cartesian philosopher René Descartes, with his famous "Cogito, ergo sum" ("I think, therefore I am"), then further isolated the mind as an entity independent of matter, implicitly suggesting that perhaps a "mind" could exist independently of a organic body.

Enlightenment philosophy led to the separation of mind and machine, paving the way for the idea that reason could be mechanized. This thinking was a direct precursor to the Industrial Revolution, which led to the emergence of cybernetics and systems engineering, disciplines that are major contributors to modern AI.

In the 20th century, with the advent of Turing 's theory of computation and the birth of computer science, the question "What does it mean to think?" found a new context. Alan Turing proposed the idea that a machine could be considered "intelligent" if it was able to mimic a human being to the point of being indistinguishable from it in a conversation test. This was the basis of the well-known " Turing Test ," a criterion still used to evaluate artificial intelligence.

Over time, the philosophy of AI has been enriched with contributions from various disciplines, including cognitive psychology, linguistics, ethics, and neuroscience. Ideas such as functionalism, which argues that what makes a mind a "mind" is more the function it performs than the matter from which it is made, opened the door to the idea that intelligence could also be made from non-biological substrates .

In more recent times, AI has raised new philosophical questions, particularly in the field of ethics and morality. With the rise of machine learning and deep learning techniques, AI is becoming increasingly autonomous, raising concerns about its potential impact on work, privacy, security and society at large.

The philosophical origins of AI are deeply rooted in centuries of inquiry into the nature of mind, reality, and existence itself. Each new discovery in AI raises further philosophical questions, making the field a continuous intersection of technology and human thought.

## The Technological Precursors (1800-1950)

Charles Babbage : In the 19th century, Charles Babbage conceived of the "Analytical Engine", which could perform complex calculations. Although it was never fully built, it is considered a forerunner of modern computers.

Alan Turing : In 1936, Turing introduced the concept of the " Turing Machine ", a theory that a machine could simulate any computational process. During World War II, Turing played a vital role in decoding the German Enigma machine.

## The Dawn of AI (1950-1970)

The 1956 Dartmouth Conference is often regarded as the birth of Artificial Intelligence (AI) as an academic and research field.

Organized by John McCarthy, Marvin Minsky , Nathaniel Rochester and Claude Shannon , the conference brought together a range of experts in several disciplines, including mathematics, engineering, and logic, at Dartmouth College in New Hampshire, USA.

The goal was to explore the possibility of building machines capable of simulating every aspect of human intelligence. In particular, proponents argued that "any aspect of learning or any other characteristic of intelligence can in principle be described so precisely as to be simulated on a computer." It was a bold statement for the time, considering the limited computing power then available and the relatively primitive understanding of human cognition.

During the conference, attendees worked on a variety of challenges, including problem solving, knowledge representation, machine learning, and computational linguistics. The event helped define the boundaries and aspirations of the new field of AI, providing a forum for the exchange of ideas and interdisciplinary collaboration.

One of the most enduring outcomes of the Dartmouth Conference was the introduction of the term "Artificial Intelligence", coined by John McCarthy.

The term then became the name of the research field that set out to build systems capable of performing tasks that, if performed by humans, would require intelligence. The conference marked the beginning of significant collaborations and the creation of dedicated AI laboratories and research centers, such as the MIT AI Lab founded by Marvin Minsky and John McCarthy shortly after the conference.

The Dartmouth Conference can be seen as an optimistic starting point that established an ambitious roadmap for AI.

While many initial expectations were overly optimistic, the themes and issues raised at the conference continue to shape the field of AI decades later.

The conference catalyzed research and innovation in the field, shaping what has become one of the most influential and dynamic fields of science and technology of the modern era.

After the Conference, the field of artificial intelligence (AI) began to gain momentum and produced some notable early successes that helped define the field. These are some of the first milestones:

- ELIZA (1964-1966): This was one of the first natural language processing programs, developed by Joseph Weizenbaum at MIT. The program emulated a Rogerian therapist and demonstrated how a computer could simulate a conversation with humans, albeit in a very rudimentary way.

- Perceptron (1957): Frank Rosenblatt created the Perceptron, a type of artificial neural network, which could learn and make simple decisions. The perceptron could be considered as the forerunner of modern neural networks.

- Dendral (1965): An early example of expert systems, Dendral was developed to assist chemists in identifying molecular structures by their spectral mass.

- SHRDLU (1968-1970): Developed by Terry Winograd , SHRDLU was a natural language processing program that could interpret and respond to commands given in a natural language in a "block world" environment.

- ID3 algorithm for inductive learning (1970): This algorithm, developed by Ross Quinlan , was one of the first machine learning algorithms and laid the foundation for algorithms like C4.5.

- MYCIN (1972): Another expert system, MYCIN, was developed to diagnose blood bacterial infections and suggest antibiotic treatments. While never used in a clinical setting, it demonstrated the potential of AI in medicine.

- Prolog (1972): Created by Alain Colmerauer and Philippe Roussel, the Prolog programming language became popular for AI applications, especially in expert systems and natural language processing.

- XCON System for Configuring Computers (Late 1970s): XCON (or R1) was one of the earliest and best known commercial expert systems. It was used to configure orders for Digital Equipment Corporation's VAX computer systems.

These early successes demonstrated the potential of AI in a variety of applications and provided a solid foundation for future development in the field. They have also helped secure the financial and academic backing needed for future research, even though the AI journey has been punctuated by periods of over-optimism followed by "AI winters," during which funding and enthusiasm for the field fell.

## The Winter of AI (1970-1980)

The AI winter of 1970-1980 represents an emblematic period for the field of artificial intelligence. Following a wave of optimism and generous funding, the discipline was faced with a number of challenges that challenged its validity and future. The initially high expectations were sunk by a series of failures, both theoretical and practical, which contributed to disillusioning not only the public but also the scientific community.

One of the first problems addressed was that of unfulfilled expectations. The early pioneers of AI predicted that machines capable of simulating every aspect of human intelligence would be developed within a few years. But when these expectations weren't met, the general enthusiasm for the discipline began to wane. The public, which had been exposed to grandiose promises, began to show signs of skepticism.

The technical limitations of the time played a crucial role in this decline. Available hardware was not powerful enough to handle the computational tasks required for advanced AI models.

Even more problematic was the theoretical problem of computational complexity, a challenge that researchers of the time were not yet able to overcome. These technical difficulties were magnified by the lack of large-scale data, which is the engine of many machine learning algorithms today.

During this period, the field of AI also came under attack from academic critics. For example, the book "Perceptrons" by Marvin Minsky and Seymour Papert offered a devastating critique of neural networks, which were one of the most promising approaches at the time. This criticism negatively impacted funding and research, shifting attention to other areas of computer science.

Adding to these challenges is the reduction in funding from government and private entities. Many research projects were put on hold and the field of AI, once considered the future of computing and technology, was relegated to a secondary role. This shift in resources and interest also affected academic training, with fewer students willing to enter a seemingly declining field.

However, this period of winter was not completely negative. It forced researchers to think more deeply about the fundamental questions of AI and to rethink the discipline's goals and approaches. This would eventually create a stronger foundation for the field's renaissance, fueled by improvements in hardware, greater data availability, and new, more effective algorithms. This period of introspection served as a much-needed break, allowing the AI community to reposition itself and prepare for the successes to come in the years to come.

## Rebirth and Growth (1980-2000)

The period from the 1980s to the early 2000s marked a significant renaissance for the field of artificial intelligence, setting the stage for the incredible developments we would see in the 21st century.

This renaissance was the result of a combination of factors including advances in hardware, availability of funding, and a return to more fundamental research methods.

The 1980s brought new computing architectures and faster microprocessors, which made previously unthinkable computational tasks possible. Personal computers became more common, which meant scientists no longer had to compete for time on expensive, centralized mainframes. This democratized access to the calculations needed for AI research, making the field more open and inclusive.

As hardware technology advanced, there was also a return to certain AI methods that had been overlooked during the so-called "AI winter". In particular, neural networks, which had been criticized and sidelined for the previous decade, began to see a resurgence. Thanks to new algorithms and growing computing power, neural networks began to show considerable potential in a range of applications, from computer vision to speech recognition.

Meanwhile, funding programs began to flourish again. Investments from government agencies and private industry began to flow back into AI research. This was partly due to the recognition that AI has the potential to revolutionize entire industries, from healthcare to industrial manufacturing. Furthermore, commercial applications began to emerge, highlighting the economic potential of AI and thus attracting further investment.

Access to huge data sets, made possible by the increasing digitization of various aspects of society, was another key factor in the AI renaissance. Machine learning, and deep learning in particular, benefits enormously from the availability of large amounts of data. This has allowed ever more sophisticated models to be trained and validated, accelerating the pace of innovation in the field.

But perhaps one of the most important factors in this resurgence was a change in the attitude of the scientific community and the public.

The defeat of world chess champion Garry Kasparov by the IBM Deep Blue computer in 1997, for example, captured the world's imagination and marked a turning point in the way people thought about artificial intelligence. It was no longer a sci-fi fantasy; it was becoming a tangible reality with real implications for the future of humanity.

Thus, the period between 1980 and 2000 was crucial in establishing AI as a legitimate and promising research field, setting the stage for the incredible advances we would see in the new millennium. It was a time when technology, funding and ambition combined in a way that brought AI out of the obscurity of its previous "winter," and re-established it as one of the most exciting and potentially transformative fields in science and technology. of engineering.

## AI Boom in the 21st Century

The boom of Artificial Intelligence in the 21st century can be traced back to a convergence of factors that have catapulted technology from the edge of academic research right into the heart of our daily lives. One of the symbolic events that mark this paradigm shift is undoubtedly the victory of AlphaGo over the world champion of Go, Lee Sedol , in 2016. This event represented much more than just a game of chess; it was a demonstration of the potential of AI to tackle and solve problems that require insights and strategies considered a uniquely human domain.

The Go match was a collective "Eureka" moment. It showed the world that Artificial Intelligence was ready to take on challenges that went far beyond computation and data analytics. The implications were immense. If an algorithm could beat a human in such a complex game, what could it do in fields like medicine, transportation or governance?

Since then, AI has continued to expand into a variety of industries. In the medical field, deep learning algorithms are revolutionizing the diagnosis and treatment of diseases. Systems like IBM's Watson are giving doctors the tools to analyze massive amounts of medical data, speeding up the diagnosis process and making treatments more accurate and effective.

The way we interact with technology has also changed. Virtual assistants like Siri and Alexa have become an integral part of our daily lives, helping us with a variety of tasks ranging from scheduling reminders to online shopping. The social and cultural implications of this integration are immense, making us reflect on fundamental issues such as privacy, security and ethics in the use of technology.

At the same time, with great opportunities come great responsibilities. The rapid adoption of AI has raised ethical and moral questions. The proliferation of facial recognition and the use of algorithms in justice systems or surveillance are raising sensitive privacy and civil rights issues. And then there is the question of work. While AI promises to automate repetitive tasks, there is concern it could replace workers in a much wider range of roles, from transportation to customer service.

But perhaps the most fascinating thing about the AI boom in the 21st century is how it forces us to reflect on ourselves as a species. AlphaGo wasn't just a product of years of research and development; it was a mirror that showed us the possibilities and limits of our intelligence, prompting us to consider the future in a way we could not have done before. On the one hand, it shows us a future full of potential, where the limits of the possible are constantly being pushed further. On the other hand, it serves us as a reminder of the ethical responsibilities that accompany this new era.

The AI boom in the 21st century is therefore much more than a technological success story; it is a story that concerns us all, which challenges us to imagine new ways of living, working and coexisting with machines. And like any great story, it's one that's still in the making, filled with opportunities, challenges, and most importantly, endless possibilities.

## The Current Importance

The role of AI in contemporary society cannot be underestimated. According to a report by the McKinsey Global Institute, AI could add up to 13 trillion dollars to the global economy by 2030. Its presence is felt in every sector: in medicine, AI algorithms are helping in the early diagnosis of diseases such as the cancer; in the financial world, high-frequency trading companies use AI to predict the slightest fluctuations in the market.

But with great power also comes great responsibility. Concerns about AI, such as bias and discrimination, have become topics of global debate. For example, in 2018, research showed that an algorithm used in the United States to guide bail decisions was prone to discriminate against minority ethnic groups.

With this overview, the goal of this book is to provide a lens through which to examine the incredibly complex world of AI, addressing not only its achievements but also its challenges. The promise of AI is immense, but as with any powerful tool, it's essential to use it wisely and with understanding.

# Chapter 2: The Birth of Artificial Intelligence

From myths and legends to the first calculators

The idea of giving life to inanimate objects is as old as the history of mankind. In ancient Greece, myths like that of Pygmalion tell of statues coming to life. In Jewish culture, the legend of the Golem speaks of a clay being animated by spells. These stories, mythic though they are, reflect a deep human desire to create and animate, to give life and intelligence.
However, the story of AI truly begins in the Renaissance, with the advent of the first mechanical machines. Leonardo da Vinci, in the fifteenth century, sketched sketches of a "mechanical man", a sort of armor animated by a complex system of gears and pulleys. But it is in the 19th century, with inventors such as Charles Babbage and his "Analytical Engine", that we see the first concrete steps towards the creation of machines capable of performing complex calculations, foreshadowing the advent of modern computers.
Charles Babbage (1791-1871) is often credited with being the "father of the computer". He was an English mathematician, mechanical engineer and inventor whose vision of automated mechanical calculations made him a pioneer in the history of computation.

First Attempts: The Differential Machine

Before the Analytical Engine, Babbage conceived of the "Differential Engine" in the 1820s. This machine was intended to produce mathematical tables. At a time when these calculations were done by hand and were prone to error, a machine that could produce accurate results was a revolutionary idea.

However, due to technical and financial complications, Babbage never completed a working version of the Differential Engine.

## The Vision of the Analytical Engine

After the Differential Engine, Babbage began work on an even more ambitious device: the Analytical Engine. Conceived in the 1830s, this machine was supposed to be capable of doing all sorts of mathematical calculations, not just producing tables.

The Analytical Engine had several notable features:

Input and Output: It was designed to read instructions and data from "punched cards," which were common in weaving at the time and which would become a standard input medium in early computers. The machine would print the results on paper or plates.

Memory and Processor: Babbage devised a " store " (an area of memory) to hold up to 1,000 numbers of 40 decimal digits and a " mill " (a processor) that would perform calculations on numbers drawn from the store .

Programmability: The most revolutionary feature was its programmability. The Analytical Engine could have performed a sequence of operations, including cycles and conditions, a fundamental capability of any modern computer.

## Collaboration with Ada Lovelace

Babbage 's most famous collaborators was Ada Lovelace , daughter of the poet Lord Byron. Lovelace is known for her writings on the work of Babbage , particularly her annotations on an article by Luigi Federico Menabrea concerning the Analytical Engine.

In his work, Lovelace wrote what is considered the first "program" for the Analytical Engine, even though the engine was never built. Because of this, Ada Lovelace is often called the "world's first programmer".

## Challenges and Legacy

Despite his vision, Babbage was never able to build a working Analytical Engine, largely due to technological limitations and lack of funding. However, Babbage 's ideas had a profound influence. The diagrams and detailed notes he left behind proved the feasibility of his design.
While actual programmable machines would not be built until a century after his death, Babbage 's Analytical Engine represents a crucial step in the history of computing and a visionary expression of what was to become the modern computer.

## Alan Turing : The Genius Who Changed the World

### Youth and Education

Alan Matison Turing was born on June 23, 1912 in London. Already at a young age, Turing showed signs of an exceptional mind, particularly inclined towards mathematics and science. Despite the traditional expectations of British schools of the time, which pushed towards classical studies, Turing persevered in his passion for numbers and logic. He continued his studies at the University of Cambridge, where he obtained a degree in mathematics. It was here that he began to formulate his revolutionary ideas about computing.

### Turing Machine and decidability

In 1936, Turing published "On Computable Numbers , with an Application to the Entscheidungsproblem ", a paper which introduced the idea of the " Turing Machine ". This was a theoretical device, a kind of abstract machine, which could simulate the operation of any given algorithm. With this tool conceptual, Turing negatively solved the famous " Entscheidungsproblem " proposed by mathematicians David Hilbert and Wilhelm Ackermann , showing that there is no universal algorithm that can determine the truth of every mathematical statement. This work, together with the parallel one by Alonzo Church, laid the foundations for the theory of computation.

War and the Decryption Machine

During World War II, Turing worked at Bletchley Park, Britain's main decryption centre. Here, he devoted himself to decoding German communications encrypted by the Enigma machine. With his genius and inventiveness, Turing devised the "Bombe", an electric machine that could speed up the decryption process.
His work, together with that of his colleagues at Bletchley Park, was fundamental for the Allies, allowing them to anticipate many German moves. Turing 's work is estimated to have shortened the duration of the war by several years, saving millions of lives.

Turing Test and the Vision of Artificial Intelligence
In 1950, Turing published "Computing Machinery and Intelligence" in the journal Mind . Here, he posed the question "Can machines think?". Instead of answering directly, he proposed an experiment, now known as the " Turing Test ", a criterion for evaluating the intelligence of machines based on their ability to mimic human intelligence.

## Personal Life and Tragic End

Turing was homosexual, a trait that was illegal in the UK at the time. In 1952, he was arrested and convicted of "gross indecency". He was offered chemical castration as an alternative to prison, and he chose that option. His conviction and subsequent treatment had a heavy impact on his personal and professional life. Tragically, Alan Turing died on June 7, 1954, under circumstances that many believe was suicide. He was only 41 years old.

Turing 's life and work had a profound and lasting impact on multiple fields, from mathematics to cryptography, philosophy to biology and, of course, computer science and artificial intelligence. Despite his tragic life and the persecution he suffered, his legacy persists as a testament to human genius and its ability to transform the world. In 2013, Queen Elizabeth II granted Turing a posthumous pardon, acknowledging the injustice done to him and honoring his invaluable contributions to science and society.

## The Dartmouth Conference and the Dawn of AI

In 1956, a small group of scientists and mathematicians gathered in the quiet town of Hanover , New Hampshire for the Dartmouth Conference. It was here that John McCarthy coined the term "Artificial Intelligence". This event marked the official start of AI as a research field.

Prior to the Dartmouth Conference, many scientific disciplines were independently exploring domains that would become central to artificial intelligence. From mathematical logic to early computers, from cybernetics to information theory, a number of ideas about machines that "think" had emerged.

In 1955, John McCarthy, a junior professor at Dartmouth University, along with Marvin Minsky , Nathaniel Rochester and Claude Shannon , proposed a summer meeting to explore these ideas. In their proposal , they wrote: "The goal of the study is to teach machines to behave in ways that, if exhibited by humans, would be called intelligent."

## The event

The bout took place during the summer of 1956 at Dartmouth College, Hanover , New Hampshire, lasting several weeks. The goal was to bring together brilliant minds from different disciplines to collaborate and set the course for AI research.
During the conference, attendees discussed a variety of topics, including machine learning, programming languages for simulating intelligence, problem solving, and even aspects of seeing and listening to machines.

## Results and Impact

It was precisely on the occasion of the Dartmouth Conference that John McCarthy coined the term "Artificial Intelligence". He opted for this terminology to distance himself from "cybernetics", a popular field of study at the time but with a broader vision that did not focus exclusively on the emulation of intelligence.
The conference was one of the first occasions where experts from different disciplines came together to explore the potential of AI. This collaborative spirit has remained a mainstay in AI research.
While many of the initial ambitions were optimistic, the conference set the agenda for AI research for decades to come. Concepts such as machine learning, which were only in a nutshell at the time, have become fundamental in today's AI landscape.

## Criticisms and Reactions

While the conference provided a platform for enthusiasm and optimism, not everyone shared the attendees' view. Some critics argued that the approach to simulating human intelligence through machines was too narrow and could not capture the complexity of human thought.

The Dartmouth Conference is often seen as the birthplace of AI as a distinct research field. While not all of the initial aspirations were realized, and there were many challenges along the way, the event undoubtedly shaped the direction and scope of AI, setting the stage for the successes and innovations we see today.

The Rise and the Fall: Enthusiasm and the "Winters" of AI

After the Dartmouth conference, there were decades of progress and setbacks. Periods of intense enthusiasm and funding were followed by "AI winters," where lack of tangible progress and technical challenges led to doubts and funding cuts.

The first wave of optimism in the 1960s and 1970s was about "expert systems." These programs, like MYCIN in the medical field, were designed to emulate human decision making in specific domains.

However, they have proved limited and difficult to scale, leading to declining enthusiasm. Despite these ups and downs, fundamental research continued, laying the groundwork for the renaissance of AI in the late 20th and early 21st centuries. , fueled by new algorithms, computing power and, above all, data.

The birth and growth of Artificial Intelligence are intrinsically linked to the evolution of our understanding of intelligence itself and our relentless aspiration to replicate and improve it. From Turing to Minsky , from ancient legends to modern algorithms, the story of AI is a fascinating journey through the dreams, challenges and realizations of the human mind.

# The Pioneers of Artificial Intelligence

While artificial intelligence has cemented itself as one of the dominant forces in technology today, its roots lie in a series of visionary individuals who dared to dream of a world in which machines could think. These AI pioneers, through their research and innovations, created the foundation upon which today's digital world is built.

## John McCarthy: The Visionary behind Artificial Intelligence

Born in 1927 in Boston, Massachusetts, John McCarthy showed an early passion for mathematics and logic. After attending Caltech , he continued his education at Princeton University , where he earned his doctorate in mathematics in 1951.

McCarthy's most famous contribution to the world of computing was undoubtedly when, in 1955, he proposed the "Dartmouth Conference", which was held the following year. This conference was instrumental in the formal emergence of AI as a field of study. It was in this context that McCarthy coined the term "Artificial Intelligence", highlighting his vision of machines capable of simulating every aspect of human intelligence.

In addition to naming the discipline, McCarthy made another significant contribution with the creation of the LISP programming language in 1958. LISP, which stands for " LISt Processing," quickly became the primary language for artificial intelligence research due to its powerful capacity for symbolic manipulation and its expressive structure. Even today, variations of LISP such as Clojure find application in many industries.

In 1965, McCarthy founded the Stanford Artificial Intelligence Laboratory (SAIL). This lab quickly became an epicenter for AI research, attracting brilliant minds from around the world.

During his time at Stanford, McCarthy further developed his ideas about programs that could emulate human intelligence.

Though less well known than his other contributions, McCarthy was one of the first to foresee a future in which computing would occur through a "utility" model, similar to electricity or water. This vision anticipated what we know today as " cloud computing".

McCarthy didn't just limit himself to the technical aspect of AI. He also reflected on the philosophical and ethical implications of intelligent machines. Among his musings was the idea that machines, in the future, could have human-like rights if they reached a certain level of consciousness.

John McCarthy was undoubtedly one of the pillars of the evolution of Artificial Intelligence. His work, from the Dartmouth Conference to the creation of LISP, laid the foundation for generations of researchers. His view of AI was not only technical, but also deeply interconnected with philosophical and ethical questions, showing the depth of his thinking and the breadth of his vision.

## Marvin Minsky : The Explorer of Artificial Intelligence

Born in 1927 in New York City, Marvin Minsky showed an early interest in mathematics, physics and, in particular, in music, in which field he showed an exceptional talent. After earning a bachelor's degree in mathematics from Harvard in 1950, Minsky received a doctorate in mathematics from Princeton in 1954.

Minsky 's major contributions to the field of AI was co-founding the MIT Artificial Intelligence Laboratory in 1959 with John McCarthy. This lab quickly became an epicenter of artificial intelligence research and trained many of the experts who would later become leaders in the field.

Marvin Minsky was one of the first to explore the idea that machines could be programmed to "think".

In 1961, he created the first learning machine neural network called SNARC (Stochastic neural analog Reinforcements Calculator), which was an early incarnation of what we now call artificial neural networks.

One of Minsky 's most influential works was "The Society of Mind" (1986), in which he proposed that intelligence does not arise from a single process or algorithm, but rather from a complex interaction of numerous small processes. This view was at odds with many theories of the time and profoundly influenced the understanding of neural networks and deep learning.

Though he contributed to the early.stages of neural networks, Minsky became critical of the limitations of deep learning, arguing that to truly realize artificial intelligence, it was necessary to explore more complex cognitive models and not just neural networks.

In addition to his works on artificial intelligence, Minsky has also made significant contributions to robotics. He developed the "confused limb," an early robotic device that simulated a human arm's ability to pick up and manipulate objects.

Minsky didn't limit himself to just the technical aspect of AI. He also thought extensively on the philosophical implications of artificial intelligence, particularly how machines might one day develop a form of consciousness or self-awareness.

Marvin Minsky , through his research, innovations and reflections, has profoundly influenced the field of artificial intelligence. His theories, often ahead of his time, have guided and challenged generations of researchers, and his impact on the field of AI will remain lasting and indelible.

### Claude Shannon : The Father of Information Theory

Born in 1916 in Petoskey , Michigan, Claude Elwood Shannon demonstrated an early affinity for mathematics and electrical engineering.

After attending the University of Michigan, he continued his education at the Massachusetts Institute of Technology (MIT), where he began to explore the world of telecommunications.

Shannon 's major contribution to science and engineering was his seminal information theory research, presented in his groundbreaking 1948 paper "A Mathematical Theory of Communication ".

In this work, he introduced the concept of "bit" as a fundamental unit of information and outlined how information could be quantified, transmitted and encoded. This theory became the basis for modern digital communication and information processing.

While Shannon is primarily known for his information theory, he has had significant intersections with Artificial Intelligence. He worked closely with Alan Turing during World War II, and the two discussed extensively the potential of calculating machines. Shannon was one of the first to theorize that machines might one day surpass human ability at certain tasks. In the 1950s, Shannon built " Theseus ", a mechanical mouse capable of autonomously navigating through a maze. This early robotics project showed his interest and vision for a future where machines could autonomously learn and adapt to their environment.

Shannon , along with John von Neumann , was instrumental in the development of game theory, a field that studies optimal decisions in situations of competition and cooperation. This theory has found applications not only in economics, but also in artificial intelligence, especially in the training of algorithms.

After a distinguished career, Shannon retired from MIT in 1978. He continued to pursue his passions, which ranged from juggling to mechanical calculating machines, until his death in 2001. His legacy lives on: his information theory remains foundational in numerous fields, from telecommunications to biology, and his reflections on AI have paved the way for generations of researchers.

Claude Shannon , often known as the "father of information theory," has made invaluable contributions to our understanding of information, communication, and computation. While his contributions to AI might seem marginal compared to other pioneers, his influence on how we think about information and computation laid the foundation upon which AI was built.

## Allen Newell and Herbert A. Simon: Innovative Duo

Collaborating to create the " Logic Theorist ", Newell and Simon presented to the world one of the first concrete demonstrations of an artificial intelligence program. Their ideas on the problem solving and cognition have shaped research for decades.

## Allen Newell

Allen Newell (1927-1992) was one of the most influential pioneers in the fields of artificial intelligence and cognitive psychology. His research has had a significant impact on the development of computer science and the understanding of human cognitive processes.

Born in San Francisco in 1927, Newell studied physics at Stanford University. During the 1950s, he worked at the RAND Corporation, a research and development organization, where he became interested in problems simulating human behavior and met Herbert A. Simon, with whom he would develop a long and productive partnership.

Important for his career was the collaboration with Herbert A. Simon with whom he formed one of the most influential partnerships in the history of AI and cognitive psychology.

Together they developed the Logic Theorist in 1956, which is often described as the first artificial intelligence program.

It was a program capable of proving mathematical logic theorems. They later created the General Problem Solver (GPS) in 1957, a computer program that aimed to solve generic problems by simulating the human thought process.

Newell was a strong believer that computers could be used to simulate all aspects of human intelligence. He has worked on "production systems" theory, which describes how knowledge is represented and used in the human brain. Newell has also proposed various models of memory and attention, significantly contributing to the understanding of these processes in cognitive psychology. The scientist spent most of his academic career at Carnegie Mellon University , where he helped establish the computer science department and the artificial intelligence research program.

For their outstanding contributions to the field of computer science and AI, Newell and Simon were awarded the prestigious Turing Award in 1975.

Allen Newell died in 1992, but his work continues to influence and inspire research in artificial intelligence, cognitive psychology, and cognitive science in general. His interdisciplinary vision, which saw the human mind as a system that could be simulated through algorithms and computational models, laid the foundations for much contemporary research in these fields.

### Herbert Alexander Simon

Herbert Alexander Simon was one of the most eclectic and influential intellectuals of the 20th century, making significant contributions to several fields, including economics, cognitive psychology, management science and computer science.

Born June 15, 1916 in Milwaukee, Wisconsin, Simon showed an early interest in science and the study of man, and received a BA in political science from the University of Chicago in 1936.

While working as a research assistant at UC Berkeley, Simon developed a growing interest in decision theory. In 1949, he joined the faculty of Carnegie Mellon University , where he remained for the rest of his career, holding roles in several departments, including psychology, computer science, and management.

Simon developed the Theory of Bounded Rationality by challenging the traditional idea of the "homo economicus " who makes perfectly rational decisions. Instead, he proposed the concept of "bounded rationality," suggesting that individuals make decisions based on incomplete information and often using heuristics rather than comprehensive analysis. He also provided profound insights into the theory of organizations and management science, arguing that organizations are complex systems that operate with bounded rationality.

Simon was awarded the Nobel Prize in Economics in 1978 for his pioneering research on the decision-making process within business organizations. In 1975, together with Allen Newell , he received the Turing Award for their outstanding contributions to artificial intelligence and cognitive psychology.

Simon died on February 9, 2001 in Pittsburgh, Pennsylvania.

His multidisciplinary legacy continues to influence and inspire in many fields. His work changed the way we understand decision, organization and cognition, and his theories continue to be central to many disciplines.

Herbert A. Simon can be defined as an intellectual giant whose work has left an indelible imprint on several fields of human study.

These are just some of the main contributions to AI born from the collaboration of the "Innovative Duo":

The Logical Limitation Theorem: Simon and Newell proposed that every agent, be it human or machine, is limited by its knowledge and processing power. This concept has become fundamental in cognitive psychology and decision theory.

The Logic Program Theorist (LT): In 1956, Newell and Simon developed the Logic Theorist , often described as the first AI program. LT was able to prove mathematical logic theorems, and many see this as the official start of AI as a research discipline.

General Problem Solver (GPS): In 1957, they created GPS, a computer program designed to solve general problems in a way similar to humans. While GPS had its limitations, it provided a critical platform for future AI research.

Human Cognition Research: In addition to their work on AI, Newell and Simon have also made significant contributions to cognitive psychology. They studied how humans solve problems, make decisions and process information.

The collaboration between Newell and Simon thus laid the foundations for modern artificial intelligence and cognitive psychology. They introduced the idea that intelligence could be understood as an algorithmic process and that machines could be programmed to emulate these abilities. Their interdisciplinary vision, which brought together computer science, psychology and economics, had a lasting and profound impact on the way we conceive of intelligence, both human and artificial.

## Frank Rosenblatt : The dream of neural networks

Frank Rosenblatt was born July 11, 1928 in New Rochelle , New York. From his youth, he shows a strong interest in science and technology.

After earning a Bachelor of Science from Cornell University in 1950, he continues to pursue his academic passion at the same institution, earning a Ph.D. in psychology in 1956.

Rosenblatt 's research leads him to make significant advances in the emerging field of artificial intelligence. While working at Cornell aeronautical Laboratory in 1957, introduces the concept of perceptron to the world.

This innovative algorithm, inspired by the biological function of neurons in the brain, is designed to recognize patterns. One of its distinguishing features is the ability to "learn" from labeled data through an iterative process of adjusting weights, marking one of the first examples of supervised learning in an artificial neural network.

Rosenblatt has high expectations for the perceptron, believing it could one day revolutionize areas such as machine translation, people or voice recognition, and perhaps even simulate complex aspects of human behavior. His vision of the future of artificial intelligence is optimistic and full of potential.

However, the initial enthusiasm for the perceptron soon met with substantial criticism. Marvin Minsky and Seymour Papert , in particular, point out some significant limitations of single-layer perceptrons in their 1969 book "Perceptrons". The resonance of these criticisms had a chilling effect on neural network research for some years.

Despite these challenges, Rosenblatt remains a passionate advocate of his ideas. Sadly, he didn't get the opportunity to see how the field of artificial intelligence would weather criticism and adopt neural networks as a core component. His life was tragically cut short by a boating accident on July 11, 1971, at the age of 43.

Rosenblatt 's untimely passing does not prevent his work from having a lasting impact. Years after his death, the importance of perceptrons and neural networks in the field of AI is recognized, affirming his status as a pioneer and visionary. His legacy lives on through the innovations that continue to form the heart of modern machine learning and artificial intelligence.

# Geoffrey Hinton: The Rebirth of Deep Learning

Geoffrey Hinton, often referred to as the 'godfather of deep learning', was born in Wimbledon, London, in 1947. Coming from a family of scientists, his path in science seemed almost predetermined. His great-grandfather was George Boole, the mathematician who invented Boolean algebra, which is central to modern information and computing theory.

Hinton began his academic training at King's College, Cambridge, where he obtained a BA in Experimental Psychology. Later, he moved to the United States to pursue a Ph.D. in Artificial Intelligence from the University of California at San Diego.

During the early 1980s, at a time when interest in neural networks was waning, Hinton continued to pursue his belief that they were the key to unlocking the secrets of human learning and perception. He collaborated with several researchers, developing concepts that would become fundamental to the field of deep learning, such as the backpropagation algorithm and deep neural networks.

In 1987, Hinton moved to Canada and began teaching at the University of Toronto. Here, he led a generation of deep learning researchers. His work in Canada led him to found the Vector Institute, a research center dedicated to artificial intelligence and machine learning.

One of Hinton's most significant contributions was in the field of unsupervised deep learning. He proposed the idea that neural networks could be trained effectively without the use of labeled data, a revolutionary prospect at the time.

Despite his rise to a leading figure in the field of AI, Hinton remained humble and committed to research. He has received numerous honors for his contributions, including the AM Turing Medal , often described as the "Nobel Prize of Computing".

Geoffrey Hinton's vision for artificial intelligence and his tireless commitment to research made possible the modern deep learning revolution. His influence in the field is invaluable, and his ideas will continue to drive the evolution of AI for many years to come.

# Chapter 3: Machine Learning Techniques

Machine learning, often thought of as a subcategory of artificial intelligence, is the art and science of building systems that can learn from data. Rather than being explicitly programmed to perform a task, these systems are trained using large amounts of data and algorithms that give them the ability to improve their performance. The basic idea is that, with enough data, experience, and iterations, a computer can discover patterns, relationships, or information that may not be immediately apparent or understandable to humans.

Imagine you have a black box that, when you give it an input, gives you an output. In a traditional software program, how this black box processes input and produces output would be determined by a set of instructions defined and coded by a programmer. In machine learning, however, this black box, or model, has no fixed instructions. Instead, it changes and adapts based on the data it encounters.

The appeal of machine learning lies in its ability to adapt, learn and improve. You can start by providing your model with a data set, known as a training set, that contains examples of the inputs you might provide and the outputs you would expect. Through an iterative process, the model "learns" how to process this data. Once the model has been trained, it can be tested on new, never-before-seen data to see how well its predictions or decisions match reality.

But what does it actually mean for a machine to "learn"? At a very high level, it means adjusting a number of internal parameters so that when given input, it produces the most accurate output possible. This process of regulation occurs through a combination of mathematics, statistics and calculation.

A concrete example might help: think of an email filter that identifies and flags spam. Instead of telling the filter exactly how to recognize spam, you could train it on thousands or millions of emails, some of which are labeled as spam and some as legitimate mail. Over time, the filter "learns" to recognize the typical characteristics of spam emails and becomes increasingly effective in marking them as such.

Machine learning represents a paradigm shift in information processing and software creation. While we once strictly defined what a computer should do step by step, we now give computers examples of what we want them to do and let them infer how to achieve those goals through the learning process. This approach has opened the door to innovations in numerous fields, from speech recognition to financial trading, from medical diagnostics to autonomous vehicles.

Machine learning is like a raging river sweeping its way through the artificial intelligence landscape, with the promise of transforming not only how we interact with machines, but also how we conceive of knowledge and discovery.

The desire to teach machines to "think" and "learn" is not new. The question of learning has been explored for centuries by philosophers, logicians and scientists. The British philosopher and mathematician George Boole, in the 19th century, introduced a form of algebra (now known as Boole's Algebra) which became the theoretical basis of digital logic and, consequently, of information processing in machines.

The fundamental theoretical question of machine learning is: how can we make a system improve its performance through experience? At first glance, this question might seem simple, but when you delve into the mechanics of learning, it becomes one of the most profound and complex questions in the field of AI.

The beating heart of machine learning is algorithms. These algorithms, such as linear regression, neural networks, or decision trees, are the rules or procedures that a machine follows to look for patterns in data. The choice of algorithm depends on the nature of the task, the quality and quantity of data available, and the desired goal.

A machine learning model, once trained, is nothing more than a representation of what it has "learned" from the data. For example, if you're trying to predict home prices based on various characteristics such as square footage, number of bedrooms, and proximity to amenities, the resulting model will be a summary of these relationships.

Machine learning, while powerful, also has its limitations. Training accurate models requires large amounts of data. Also, there is always the risk of "overfitting," where a model might perform exceptionally well on the data it was trained with, but fail miserably on new data.

There is also the question of interpretability. While some models can be easily interpreted and understood, others, such as deep neural networks, are often described as "black boxes" as it is difficult to understand exactly how they are making their decisions.

The future of machine learning is as exciting as it is uncertain. We're already seeing the rise of deep learning, a subclass of machine learning that uses deep neural networks and is making breakthroughs in fields like image recognition and natural language. At the same time, awareness of the importance of ethics in machine learning is growing. Issues such as bias and discrimination in models are becoming central concerns.

Machine learning is a combination of mathematics, logic, computing and philosophy. Its ability to transform raw data into insights and knowledge represents one of the most exciting frontiers of modern science and technology.

## Supervised learning

Supervised learning is one of the fundamental pillars of machine learning, and its essence lies in the very term "supervised".

In this mode, machines are trained on a dataset that has been labeled, i.e. each data instance supplied to the model is accompanied by a label or desired outcome. The model's job is then to learn the relationship between the input data and its corresponding labels so that, once the training is complete, it can make accurate predictions about new, unlabeled data.

Imagine you want to train a system to recognize if a photo contains a cat or a dog. In a supervised learning context, you would feed the system a set of images where each image is clearly labeled "cat" or "dog". Through iterations and examining many examples, the system would try to hone its recognition capabilities. Thus, once trained, if given a new picture of an animal it has never seen before, it could predict with some accuracy whether the picture represents a cat or a dog based on learning from the training data.

Supervised learning has gained considerable popularity in contemporary research and has led to significant advances in multiple areas. One of them is the medical diagnosis. Recently, there have been significant efforts in training models to recognize signs and symptoms of disease from medical images. For example, researchers have trained supervised learning models using chest X-ray images to detect signs of conditions such as pneumonia. The images used for training were labeled by medical experts, thus allowing the model to learn the visual characteristics of the disease. Once trained, these models showed remarkable accuracy in detecting pneumonia on new radiography images.

Another notable example of supervised learning in contemporary research is machine translation. For example, systems like Google Translate have benefited from supervised learning. Researchers train these models by feeding them large amounts of bilingual text, where a sentence in one language is matched with its translation in another language. This allows the system to "learn" the linguistic structures and nuances between languages, improving the quality of translations for sentences or texts never seen before.

In summary, supervised learning is a methodology that harnesses the power of labeled data to teach machines how to make accurate predictions. While the examples provided represent only the tip of the iceberg, they highlight the revolutionary potential of this technique in tackling complex problems across a wide range of industries.

Supervised learning doesn't just stop at categorizing images or translating text. It is a vast sphere of techniques and methodologies that can be applied to a myriad of problems, where the main objective is to predict or estimate a particular output based on one or more inputs.

In a more formal definition, supervised learning involves a set of training data composed of inputs together with their corresponding desired outputs. The goal is to infer a function from this training data. Once this function has been determined, it can be used to map new inputs to expected outputs.

Consider, for example, the weather forecast. A supervised learning model could be trained on years of historical weather data: temperatures, humidity, barometric pressure, etc. (the inputs), along with the corresponding weather condition that actually occurred, such as sunshine, rain, snow (the outputs). . With enough data and training, the model could begin to recognize atmospheric patterns that precede a particular weather event and accurately predict future conditions.

However, like all techniques, supervised learning has its challenges. The quality and quantity of labeled data is critical. If the training data is incorrect or biased, the model produced will be equally unreliable. This concept is commonly known as " garbage in, garbage out" in AI.

Another important consideration is generalization. While our model might work perfectly with data it was trained on, the real test is how well it performs on never-before-seen data. If a model is too "tight" on the training data, it may not perform well on new data, a phenomenon known as "overfitting". Additionally, supervised learning requires experts to provide labels for training data, a process that can be costly and time-consuming. In many contexts, obtaining a large set of accurately labeled data can be a challenge.

Despite these challenges, supervised learning has revolutionized numerous industries. From finance to biomedicine, from agriculture to logistics, the ability to predict outcomes based on historical data has opened up new frontiers of efficiency, precision and insight . And as new techniques and paradigms continue to emerge, supervised learning remains a staple in the AI repertoire, shaping the way we live, work, and interact with the world around us.

## Unsupervised learning

Unsupervised learning is a distinctive and fascinating category of machine learning. Unlike supervised learning, where a model is trained on labeled data, unsupervised learning works with unlabeled data, trying to identify intrinsic structures and patterns in them without specific guidance as to what those structures represent.

One way to understand unsupervised learning is to think of it as an exploratory process. Without having specific labels as a reference, models try to group or segment data based on similarities or differences.

This exploration can reveal hidden relationships in the data that may not be immediately apparent or would not have been considered using supervised techniques.

A concrete example of unsupervised learning is clustering , where the goal is to group similar data together. Consider a large set of data about customers' online shopping. A company might not know how to segment its customers in advance, but using unsupervised learning techniques, it could discover natural groups of customers based on their shopping habits, the categories of products they like, or how often they buy.

Another approach in unsupervised learning is dimensionality reduction . This technique tries to simplify complex data by reducing the number of variables considered, while retaining most of the original information. A well-known example in this context is principal component analysis (PCA). Recently, techniques such as the autoencoder , particularly popular in deep neural networks, have been used to compress and then recreate data, resulting in denser and more informative representations.

One of the most intriguing examples of contemporary research in unsupervised learning is the use of Generative Adversarial Networks (GANs). Without going into too much technical detail, GANs consist of two networks: one that generates data and one that tries to distinguish real data from generated data. This competitive game between the two networks leads to the creation of extremely realistic synthetic data. GANs have found applications in a variety of fields, from creating fine art images to synthetic medical images for research.

Another area of research that takes advantage of unsupervised learning is text analysis.

embedding templates such as Word2Vec or FastText try to convert words into number vectors so that words with similar meanings are close together in vector space. This transformation is accomplished by observing how words coexist in large bodies of text, without any specific labeling.

In conclusion, unsupervised learning offers a unique opportunity to probe and analyze data without the need for predefined labels. It opens doors to new discoveries and insights, allowing machines to reveal patterns and structures that we may not have considered or that may be too complex to identify through human analysis. Through its ability to work with unconditioned data, unsupervised learning remains one of the most promising and rapidly evolving areas of artificial intelligence.

Unsupervised learning has found application in a number of domains revolutionizing the way we interact with technology and understand the world around us.

One particularly fascinating area is the conjunction between art and technology. For example, Generative Adversarial Networks (GAN) have broken new ground in artistic creation. "Edmond de Belamy " is a testament to this: a portrait which, although created by an algorithm and not by the hand of an artist, was sold at an auction at Christie's for a significant sum, raising questions about the very essence of the art.

In the music industry, platforms like Spotify and Apple Music are redefining the listener experience. These services, using unsupervised learning, analyze users' listening habits and offer music that, although they have never been heard before, are in tune with the user's tastes. The personalization achieved offers an almost bespoke musical experience, reflecting the singularity of each listener.

In the fast-paced world of e-commerce, analyzing consumer behavior is key. Using unsupervised learning techniques, companies are able to group customers based on purchasing behavior, products viewed, or site visit times. This segmentation allows for customization of offers and targeted advertising, enhancing customer confidence and increasing the likelihood of a sale.

Cybersecurity is another domain that benefits greatly from these techniques. Every day, huge amounts of data pass through our systems and networks. Using unsupervised learning, this data can be monitored for anomalous behavior or patterns, providing a first level of defense against possible threats or intrusions.

In the field of computational linguistics, the last few years have seen extraordinary progress thanks to models such as BERT or GPT-2. Working on large volumes of text, these models are able to generate and understand human language with unprecedented accuracy. This has led to dramatic improvements in areas such as machine translation, speech recognition and text understanding.

Biomedical and pharmaceutical research is also profoundly influenced by these technologies. For example, analyzing genomic sequences or medical images with unsupervised learning can reveal patterns or structures that would escape traditional analysis, offering new insights into diagnoses or treatments. In the field of pharmaceutical research, the generation of new molecules through GAN accelerates the process of developing new drugs, reducing costs and potentially saving lives.

Unsupervised learning is more than just a technological tool: it is shaping our future, offering innovative solutions to age-old problems and opening new horizons in hitherto unexplored areas.

## Reinforcement learning

Reinforcement learning is one of the most intriguing offshoots of machine learning, as it simulates the process by which humans and animals learn through interaction with their environment. In this paradigm, an agent makes decisions by exploring an environment, receiving "reinforcements" or rewards for his or her actions. The agent's goal is to maximize the reward accumulated over time.

Unlike supervised learning, where teaching is through corrected examples, or unsupervised learning, which tries to find structures in data, reinforcement learning focuses on how to perform actions in an environment to get the maximum benefit.

One of the most celebrated examples of reinforcement learning in the modern era is AlphaGo , developed by DeepMind , a subsidiary of Google. AlphaGo surprised the world by defeating world champions in the complex game of Go, a challenge many thought beyond the reach of computers due to its strategic depth. AlphaGo learned by studying human games and then playing countless games against itself, honing its strategies through reinforcement learning.

In addition to games, reinforcement learning has found application in robotics, where robots learn how to move and interact with the physical world through experimentation and correction.

For example, robots learning to walk or grasp objects often use reinforcement learning to optimize their movements.

And what does the future hold for us? We could see an increase in the use of reinforcement learning in the optimized management of energy resources. Imagine intelligent systems that regulate energy consumption in cities in real time, learning from environmental conditions and consumption patterns to ensure efficient use of energy. Or, we could have autonomous vehicles that use reinforcement learning to improve safety and efficiency in traffic by adapting to road conditions and the behavior of other road users.

In the field of medicine, systems guided by reinforcement learning could assist doctors in choosing treatments. Instead of relying solely on clinical experience or standard protocols, these systems could suggest treatments based on deep analysis of patient data, getting real-time feedback and tailoring recommendations accordingly.

Such learning has the potential to bring AI to a wide range of applications, prompting systems to dynamically adapt, learn and optimize in response to real-world challenges. And while we already see impressive applications today, the future may hold even more revolutionary solutions that transform the way we live, work and interact with technology.

Reinforcement Learning (RL) is based on a mathematical formalism that represents the interaction between an agent and an environment, called the Markov Decision Process ( MDP ). In an MDP, an agent performs actions in specific states of the environment and receives rewards (or punishments) in response. The goal is to find a policy, i.e. a strategy, that maps each state into an action, maximizing the total expected reward over time.

The heart of reinforcement learning is the value function. There are two main value functions in the RL:

- The state value function $V(s)$, representing the total expected reward from state $s$ following a certain policy.

- The action value function $Q(s, a)$, which represents the total reward expected by performing action $a$ in state $s$ and then following a certain policy.

The estimation and optimization of these functions are central to RL. Algorithms such as Q-learning and SARSA are model-free methods that try to approximate the $Q$ *function* directly through experience.

More modern approaches to RL use deep neural networks to approximate these value functions, resulting in Deep Reinforcement Learning ( DRL). These methods, such as DQN (Deep Q-Network), combine the power of deep neural networks with the principles of RL, allowing agents to operate in environments with huge state spaces, such as video games or robotic simulation.

A key concept in RL is the balance between exploration and exploitation. The agent must decide whether to explore new stocks in search of higher rewards or exploit stocks that they already know are beneficial. This is often governed by a parameter called an epsilon, which determines how likely the agent will choose a random action (exploration) versus an action that maximizes the expected reward (exploitation).

Another fundamental technical aspect is the " reward shaping ". The design of rewards is crucial in RL: if the agent receives inappropriate or misleading feedback, he can learn suboptimal or even harmful policies.

In recent years, transfer learning and meta learning techniques are gaining traction in RL. The idea is that an agent can transfer what it has learned in one task to new related tasks, significantly reducing the learning time.

Simulation has become an essential component in RL. Platforms like OpenAI Gym offer simulated environments where agents can learn without interacting with the real world, reducing the costs and risks associated with learning through direct interaction.

In summary, while reinforcement learning is based on fundamental mathematical principles and well-defined formulas, its practical application is an active and rapidly evolving area of research, with new discoveries and methodologies emerging on a regular basis.

## Semi-supervised learning

Semi-supervised learning represents a middle ground between supervised and unsupervised learning. While in supervised learning we use a labeled dataset to teach our model to make predictions or classifications, and in unsupervised learning we let the model find structures or patterns in the data without any references, semi-supervised learning falls in between, leveraging both labeled and unlabeled data.

Think of a situation where you have a large volume of data at your disposal, but only a small portion of it is tagged. Labeling data can be expensive, time-consuming, or require domain experts. In these contexts, semi-supervised learning becomes particularly useful.

The way it works is quite intuitive. Initially, the model is trained on the available labeled data, just like in supervised learning. Once the model has some understanding of the task, it is exposed to the unlabelled data. Here, the model tries to use the knowledge gained from the supervised phase to make some assumptions or predictions about the unlabelled data. These predictions are then used to further train and refine the model. The idea is that even if labels are not present for all data, the model can still derive useful information from the structure and distribution of the unlabelled data.

A practical example of semi-supervised learning can be found in text classification. Imagine you have an archive of newspaper articles, but only a small fraction of them are categorized under topics like "politics," "sports," or "business." After training your model on the small subset of tagged items, you could use semi-supervised learning to help the model identify and categorize untagged items, based on content similarity or other characteristics extracted from the tagged data.

convolutional neural networks , for image classification. Even though only a small subset of the images were labeled, the model, through semi-supervised learning techniques, was able to significantly improve its ability to classify new images compared to using labeled data alone.

In general, semi-supervised learning is a powerful solution to problems where labels are scarce or expensive to obtain, allowing models to learn more effectively and to take advantage of the large amount of unlabelled data that is often available.

# Transfer Learning

Transferable learning, also known as transfer learning, is a machine learning strategy that leverages knowledge gained from a previously learned task to enhance training in a new, related task. This approach has become particularly popular in the field of deep learning, where training deep neural networks from scratch can require large amounts of data and computational resources.

Imagine you have an image recognition model that has been trained on millions of images to recognize thousands of different objects. This model has already learned a wide range of visual features and concepts, such as borders, textures , shapes, and perhaps even more complex concepts such as "animality" or "artificial objects". If we now wanted to train a model to specifically recognize various types of plants, rather than starting from scratch, we could exploit the knowledge already acquired from the previous model, adapting it to our new specific task.

In transfer learning, you typically take a pre -trained model, often on a large dataset such as ImageNet in the case of computer vision, and modify the bottom layer or layers of the network to suit the new task. These "custom" layers are then trained on the new dataset , while the initial parts of the model can be "frozen" to retain previously acquired knowledge or undergo more light training.

A contemporary example of Transfer Learning is represented by its application in the field of medicine.

For example, neural networks pre -trained for generic object recognition can be tailored to recognize specific anomalies in medical images, such as tumors in an X-ray. Since collecting a large dataset of labeled medical images can be difficult and expensive, leveraging a pre -trained model can dramatically speed up the training process and improve performance, even with a small dataset size.

Another context where Transfer Learning is gaining ground is in Natural Language Processing (NLP). Pre -trained language models , such as BERT or GPT, have been trained on huge corpuses of text and can be adapted to specific tasks, such as sentiment analysis or document classification, with impressive results.

Transferable learning represents an efficient approach to leverage knowledge acquired in one domain or task to benefit another related domain or task, reducing the need for large amounts of data and computational resources.

## The Learning Ensemble

Ensemble learning, translatable into Italian as "learning together", is a technique in the field of machine learning that combines the predictions of multiple models in order to produce a more accurate and stable final prediction than the one that could be produced by a single model. Rather than relying on the perspective or potential of a single algorithm, Ensemble learning capitalizes on diversity, leveraging a multitude of views and approaches to approach any given problem.

A metaphor for understanding how Ensemble learning works could be that of a committee of experts. If each of these experts has slightly different training and experience, bringing them all together to make a decision could lead to better results than if a single expert decides alone. This is because the mistakes or shortcomings of one expert could be compensated for by the skills of another.

A common technique used in ensemble learning is " bagging " (Bootstrap Aggregating ), in which different versions of a dataset are created through random sampling with replacement and then a model is trained on each of these versions.

These models are then combined to produce a final prediction. A well-known example of this approach is the random forest, or "Random Forest ", which is essentially a set of decision trees.

Another popular method is " boosting ". While in bagging each model is trained in parallel and independently of the others, in boosting the models are trained sequentially, where each successive model tries to correct the errors of the previous model.

In the contemporary context, Ensemble techniques have become fundamental in many practical applications of machine learning. For example, in Kaggle competitions , a data science competition platform, many of the best results are achieved by combining different models through Ensemble techniques.

A practical example of using Ensemble learning is in forecasting the weather. Since meteorology is a highly complex and variable field, forecasters often rely on various simulations and models to arrive at a more accurate and reliable forecast.

In finance, Ensemble techniques can be used to model and predict stock market movements, combining different techniques and models to try to capture complex market dynamics.

Ultimately, Ensemble Learning recognizes and builds on the principle that "the whole is greater than the sum of its parts," combining different strategies and models to achieve robust and accurate predictions.

## Deep Neural Networks (Deep Learning)

Deep Neural Networks, often referred to as "Deep Learning", represent a subcategory of machine learning. They are based on structures composed of many layers, hence the word "deep", and are inspired by the functioning of neurons in the human brain.

These neural networks are composed of units, called artificial neurons, organized into successive layers: an input layer, various hidden layers and an output layer. The "depth" of these networks refers to the number of hidden layers they contain.

Each neuron receives an input, processes it through an activation function and produces an output, which is then passed on to the next level. During the learning process, the network changes the weights associated with each link between neurons to reduce the error between the expected and desired output.

Deep learning has gained notoriety in recent years for its ability to tackle large-scale and complex problems, often outperforming other traditional machine learning techniques. The rise of deep learning has been made possible by the massive amounts of data available for training and growing computational capabilities, especially through the use of GPUs for parallel processing.

Modern examples of the use of Deep Neural Networks include:

Computer Vision: The ability to recognize and classify objects in images is one of the most remarkable applications of Deep Learning.

Services like the automatic photo- tagging offered by Facebook or the facial recognition used for unlocking modern cell phones rely on this.

Natural Language Processing (NLP): Models like BERT, GPT-3 and others, based on deep neural networks, are revolutionizing the way machines understand and generate language. These models power services such as chatbots , automatic translators and recommendation systems.

Autonomous Vehicles: Deep neural networks underpin autonomous driving systems, allowing cars to "see" and interpret their surroundings, recognizing road signs, pedestrians, other vehicles and obstacles.

Medical Diagnosis: The use of deep learning in analyzing medical images is gaining traction, enabling the identification of tumors, abnormalities and other conditions with accuracy often exceeding that of a trained human eye.

Content Creation: Recently, there have been examples of art and music being generated by neural networks. These systems can create images, musical compositions, and even stories based on patterns learned from training data.

Deep Neural Networks are redefining what is possible in artificial intelligence, finding applications in nearly every industry and offering solutions to problems previously considered insurmountable for machines.

The appeal and power of deep neural networks lies not only in their ability to deal with huge volumes of data, but also in their flexibility to adapt to a wide range of applications and problems.

Unlike traditional machine learning algorithms, which often require fine feature engineering and can be highly specialized for specific data types or tasks, deep neural networks have the ability to autonomously "learn" relevant features from training data .

However, despite their successes and popularity, understanding the challenges and limitations of deep learning is also critical:

Need for large volumes of data: One of the main strengths of deep neural networks is their ability to work with large data sets. However, this can also be seen as a weakness, as not all applications or industries have the huge volumes of annotated data needed for training.

Interpretability: Neural networks are often criticized for being "black boxes". This means that while they are capable of producing accurate predictions, understanding how they reached a particular decision can be difficult, if not impossible. This poses problems in fields such as medicine or finance, where it is essential to understand how a decision is made.

Overfitting: Due to their complexity and depth, neural networks can fall into the trap of overfitting, i.e. overfitting to training data at the expense of generalizing to new data. However, there are techniques like dropout or regularization that have been developed to mitigate this problem.

Resource intensive: Deep learning is notoriously resource intensive. Deep model training requires specialized hardware, such as GPUs or TPUs, and can be time-consuming, especially for very large datasets or complex architectures.

Despite these challenges, the impact of deep learning on the modern world is undeniable. Consider, for example, the health sector. In addition to analyzing medical images, deep neural networks are used to predict the onset of disease based on clinical data, to assist surgeons during operations through augmented reality, or to personalize treatments for patients based on genetic profiles.

Another rapidly evolving field thanks to deep learning is robotics. Modern robots use deep learning to navigate autonomously, recognize objects, interact with humans, and even learn new skills through simulation and exploration.

Finally, deep learning has a profound impact on art and creativity. On the one hand, artists and creatives are experimenting with neural networks to produce new art forms, on the other, companies like Adobe are integrating deep learning capabilities into their software, allowing designers to accomplish tasks that were once unthinkable.

Ultimately, while deep learning has its challenges and limitations, its ability to transform industries and create new opportunities makes it one of the most powerful and promising tools in the modern AI arsenal.

These are just some of the main machine learning techniques. The field is vast and constantly evolving, with new methods and approaches emerging on a regular basis. Choosing the right technique depends on the type of problem, the nature of the data, and the specific goals of the project.

# Classification and regression algorithms

Classification and regression algorithms are two of the main categories of machine learning algorithms.

Classification algorithms are used to predict a category (or class) label for a given entry. The classification task refers to the process of assigning a certain income to one of the predefined categories. In other words, the expected response is discrete rather than continuous.

Example: Imagine that you have a set of fruit images and your goal is to identify whether an image represents an apple, a banana or an orange. Using a classification algorithm, you could train a model with labeled images of each fruit. Once trained, the model could take an image of unknown fruit and classify it into one of the categories based on its characteristics.

Regression algorithms, on the other hand, are used to predict a continuous value based on the inputs provided. Instead of providing a discrete answer as in classification, regression provides a continuous answer.

Example: Suppose you want to predict the selling price of a home based on various factors such as square footage, number of rooms, age of construction, etc. A regression algorithm would take these factors as inputs and predict a continuous value (the price of the house) as the output.

It is important to note that despite their differences, classification and regression share many common techniques and methods. For example, linear regression is a popular regression algorithm, but with some modifications, it can also be used for classification, as is the case with logistic regression.

Another point to consider is that the choice between classification and regression often depends on the nature of the problem and the type of data available. In some situations, it might be useful to convert a regression problem to a classification problem or vice versa, depending on practical needs or data limitations.

In the contemporary landscape, these algorithms are widely used in a wide range of applications, from predicting stock market trends, to medical diagnosis, to recommending products in e-commerce sites.

With the advent of big data and growing computing power, the capabilities and accuracy of these methods continue to improve, making their applications even more valuable across a variety of industries. Classification algorithms are often used when the desired output is a category. However, the nature and complexity of the problem can vary widely. Further classification can be binary, where there are only two classes (for example, "spam" or "not spam"), or multiclass , where there are three or more categories (for example, identifying the type of fruit in an image ).

Class Balance: In some cases, one class might have many more instances than another. This class imbalance can make it difficult for a model to learn the characteristics of minority classes. Techniques like oversampling , undersampling or using advanced metrics like ROC curve can help deal with these issues.

Here are some examples of use:

Facial Recognition: Classification plays a key role in determining a person's identity in an image. Here, each person could be considered a distinct class.

Sentiment Analysis : Based on the content of a review, a ranking algorithm can determine whether the sentiment is positive, negative, or neutral.

In the context of machine learning, regression is about predicting continuous values.

Characteristics:

Linearity: While linear regression assumes a linear relationship between the independent and dependent variables, there are models, such as polynomial regression, that can accommodate nonlinear relationships.

Overfitting and Underfitting : Regression can suffer from these problems.

Overfitting occurs when the model is overly complex and fits the training data too well.

Underfitting occurs when the model is too simple to capture the structure of the data . Techniques such as regularization can help combat overfitting.

Modern examples:

Predicting House Prices: Based on variables such as square footage, number of rooms, proximity to amenities, etc., a regression model can predict the selling price of a home.

Energy Demand Management: Energy companies can use regression algorithms to predict future electricity demand based on variables such as season, forecasted temperature, and historical trends.

In both cases, classification and regression, the ability to interpret results and understand the importance of each input variable is critical. This helps not only in forecasting, but also in understanding the underlying mechanisms that drive predictions, allowing for greater transparency and confidence in machine learning models.

## The Feature Engineering

The " Feature Engineering , or feature engineering, is a critical step in processing and preparing data for machine learning modeling. It is essentially a creative and often insight-driven process, where features ) of data are modified, combined or created from scratch in order to improve the performance of a model.This process can have a significant impact on the quality and effectiveness of the resulting models.

To understand the importance of the feature engineering , we could think of data as the raw material and features as the ingredients that emerge from this raw material, ready to be used in a machine learning recipe.

A good selection and transformation of features can make the "recipe" much more effective.

An example can further clarify the concept: let's imagine we have a dataset that contains the date and time when users visit an online store. From this single data, we can extract many useful features , such as the day of the week, the time of the day, whether it is a public holiday or not, etc. These new features could help us better understand user behavior patterns, such as the tendency to buy more on weekends than on weekdays.

The feature engineering can be particularly crucial when dealing with unstructured data such as text or images. In the case of text, for example, we may want to transform sentences or documents into sets of words, count the frequency of words, or use more advanced techniques such as TF-IDF ( Term Frequency -Inverse Document Frequency ) or word embeddings such as Word2Vec. In the case of images, we may want to extract borders, dominant colors or use more complex representations derived from neural networks.

One of the main challenges of the feature engineering is to avoid overfitting. By creating many new features , you run the risk of fitting the model too tightly to the training data, making it less effective on unseen new data.

The feature engineering is as much an art as a science, and often requires in-depth knowledge of the application domain. Good feature engineering can make the difference between a mediocre model and an extraordinarily effective one.

Feature engineering, or " feature engineering ", is a pillar of machine learning and can be compared to the art of sculpting: Just as a sculptor shapes raw material to reveal its hidden beauty, a data scientist transforms raw data to extract relevant information that can feed and optimize models.

In an increasingly digitized society, data can come from a variety of sources, such as IoT sensors , social media platforms, mobile devices and much more. The breadth and complexity of the data make the feature engineering a discipline that is not only necessary, but also constantly evolving.

Take, for example, the growing field of Natural Language Processing (NLP). With the rise of chatbots , virtual assistants, and recommender systems, text analytics has become central. In this context, transforming a sentence or document into a form that a machine learning model can understand is a challenge. Modern techniques, such as word embeddings (such as Word2Vec or BERT), have revolutionized the way text is represented, allowing models to capture semantic and contextual relationships between words.

Another area of application concerns images. The advent of deep neural networks, in particular the Convolutional ones Neural Networks (CNN), has radically changed the approach to the feature engineering in this sector. Instead of having to manually extract features such as edges, shapes or textures , these networks are able to automatically learn relevant features directly from the raw data during the training process.

In the field of temporal or sequential data, such as financial or weather data, creating "time windows" or data differentiation to capture trends and seasonalities are key techniques. Here, models such as LSTM (Long Short- Term Memory) or GRU ( Gated Recurrent Units ) are gaining popularity for their ability to capture long-term time dependencies.

But while automated techniques and modern network architectures have simplified many aspects of the feature engineering , the importance of domain knowledge cannot be underestimated. Effective feature engineering often requires a deep understanding of the problem at hand, the industry, and the data itself. The combination of human intuition and computational power leads to the best results, enabling machine learning models to achieve optimal performance and deliver valuable insights from data.

# Chapter 4: Neural Networks and Deep Learning: A Guide to the Cognitive Revolution

The complexity and efficiency of the human brain, with its network of billions of interconnected neurons, has always fascinated and piqued the curiosity of scientists. This structure, despite its microscopic size, is capable of tasks ranging from the recognition of visual patterns to the processing of emotions and memories. Its incredible ability to learn from experience and adapt has prompted computer scientists to ask, "What if we could replicate this network in a computer?"

The beginning of the answer to this question is found in artificial neural networks. These are basically attempts to emulate, on a much smaller scale, the structure of neurons and synapses in the brain. They are not an exact copy of biology, but rather a simplified representation, based on mathematical functions and algorithms that mimic the way neurons are thought to process and transmit information. These networks are made up of nodes (called "artificial neurons") that receive, process and send information, just like a biological neuron. When these networks "learn", this means that they are optimizing their connection weights based on the input data, trying to improve their predictions or their performance on the assigned task.

However, the leap from neural networks to deep learning was a watershed moment. While neural networks may have a limited number of layers of neurons, deep learning takes advantage of "deep" networks, with many layers.

This depth allows much more complex information to be captured and represented.

In practice, the more layers a network has, the more it can extract detailed and refined characteristics from the data.

For example, in image recognition, early layers might identify simple edges and colors, while later layers might recognize shapes, and even deeper layers might identify complex objects or even concepts.

Deep learning is revolutionizing many industries. Its capabilities to recognize patterns, learn from massive amounts of data and make accurate predictions make it ideal for applications ranging from medical diagnosis to facial recognition, automatic language translation to autonomous driving.

While the human brain remains a mystery in many of its functions, its role as a muse for the world of artificial intelligence is indisputable. And with each new discovery in neural networks and deep learning, we get one step closer to replicating, and perhaps one day surpassing, some of the extraordinary capabilities of our most complex organ.

## The Birth of Neural Networks: From Biology to Computer Science

Artificial neural networks, as we know them today, have their roots in biology and an understanding of how the human brain processes information. Although their history spans many decades, interest in creating a machine that could replicate human cognitive functions dates back to at least the early 20th century. But how did this fascinating adventure begin?

### Biological foundations and first hypotheses

The first step towards understanding the brain was taken by biologists. In 1943, Warren McCulloch and Walter Pitts published a seminal article titled "A Logical Calculus of the Ideas Immanent in Nervous Activity". In this work, they presented a simplistic mathematical model of how neurons in the brain might work.

Using logic and equations, they attempted to explain how neurons could, theoretically, perform logical and mathematical operations. Their model proposed that neurons operate as binary units, receiving input, processing it, and producing an output, either activating or not activating the neuron. This work laid the foundations for the development of artificial neural networks.

## First experiments and limits

Inspired by the work of McCulloch and Pitts , many researchers began experimenting with these concepts during the 1950s and 1960s. One of the best known examples from this period is Frank Rosenblatt 's "Perceptron" , a type of artificial neural network designed for binary classification. Although a simplified model, the Perceptron demonstrated that it was possible to train a machine to learn and make predictions using input data.

However, the initial enthusiasm for the perceptron and other similar models was tempered by a growing awareness of their limitations. In 1969, Marvin Minsky and Seymour Papert published "Perceptrons," a book that illustrated the limitations of these models, especially their inability to learn nonlinearly separable functions. This criticism cooled interest in neural networks for a few years.

Despite the obstacles, neural network research continued, albeit at a slower pace. A key breakthrough came in the 1980s with the introduction of the backpropagation algorithm , which allowed multilayer neural networks to learn from mistakes and adjust connection weights effectively. This development reopened the door to interest and investment in the field of neural networks.

The combination of these advances with the increase in computing power and the advent of large amounts of available data has led to the modern era of neural networks and deep learning, in which these systems are able to handle tasks of great complexity, often surpassing human capabilities in specific applications.

The birth of neural networks is the result of a tortuous path, in which biology, mathematics and computer science met, collided and finally collaborated to create machine learning tools of extraordinary power.

## The architecture of a neural network

Artificial neural networks are often compared to how the human brain works, not because they work exactly like our neuronal system, but rather because of the way they process information through a series of interconnected nodes or "neurons". The architecture of a neural network defines how these neurons are organized and how they interact with each other.

Let's start with the basic concept: the artificial neuron. It is a simple processing unit that takes various inputs, processes them and produces an output. Each input has an associated "weight", which determines how much that particular input affects the output. These weights are adapted and optimized during the learning process. We think of a neuron as a filter: it can give more importance to some inputs than others based on weights.

Take, for example, a neural network used to recognize pictures of cats. One neuron could be trained to detect ear shapes, while another could focus on fur color. If the input image has a cat-ear-like feature, the corresponding neuron will have high firing.

Neural networks are organized in layers. There are three main types of layers:

Input layer: It is the initial point of the network, where the raw data or characteristics to be processed are entered. If we think about image recognition, each neuron in this layer could represent a pixel of the image.

Hidden layers: They are the intermediate layers between the input and the output. Here, the magic happens. The hidden layers contain neurons that process the features detected by the previous layers, building ever more complex representations of the data. In the case of cat recognition, the first hidden layers could detect edges or colors, while later layers could recognize complex shapes such as paws or eyes.

Output layer: This layer produces the final result of the network. Depending on the specific application, it can have one or more units. For image classification, for example, each neuron could represent a different category (cat, dog, rabbit), and the unit with the highest firing would indicate the prediction of the network.

Each neuron uses an activation function to transform the weighted sum of the inputs into an output. This function can vary, but functions such as the sigmoid , hyperbolic tangent, or ReLU ( Rectified Linear Unit) are often used . These features introduce nonlinearities into the network, allowing the architecture to learn and represent complex relationships in the data.

The architecture of neural networks has evolved rapidly, with models such as CNNs ( Convolutional Neural Networks), optimal for image recognition, and RNN ( Recurrent Neural Networks), ideal for sequential data such as text or time series. For example, services like Google Photos use neural networks to categorize and recognize faces and objects in photos.

The architecture of a neural network determines its ability to learn and represent. While the basic principle remains the same, continued innovation in this field is expanding the possibilities of what these networks can do, revolutionizing industries like computer vision, machine translation, and more.

# From neural networks to deep learning

Deep learning, or deep learning, has acquired this denomination precisely because of the depth of the neural networks it employs. In this context, "depth" does not refer to a philosophical or conceptual analysis, but rather to the actual number of hidden layers present in a neural network. When we talk about a "deep neural network", we refer to a neural network with many layers, often tens or hundreds, which allow it to model extremely complex functions and capture intricate patterns in the data.

A classic example of this type of complex modeling is found in convolutional neural networks (CNNs). These networks are particularly suited to image recognition. In the early layers, a CNN can detect simple visual patterns such as borders or colors. As one moves through the successive layers, the network begins to identify more complex structures, such as shapes, textures , and eventually whole objects. A model like ResNet , for example, used for image classification, can have over 150 slices, allowing it to identify and categorize a huge range of images with extraordinary accuracy.

However, the depth of neural networks introduces new challenges. One of the main ones is the problem of gradient disappearance. When training a neural network, optimization algorithms are used that adjust the weights of neurons based on a value called a "gradient". This value indicates how much you need to change the weights to improve network performance. In deep models, the gradient can become very small, almost non-existent, as it back-propagates through each layer, making the initial weights update almost zero. This phenomenon hampers the network's ability to learn and requires innovative techniques to be overcome.

Recent developments have led to various solutions to this problem. The introduction of ReLU ( Rectified Linear Unit) activation functions and its variants helped keep gradients from disappearing or exploding.

Furthermore, initiatives such as initialization of weights and normalization techniques, such as "Batch Normalization ", have helped stabilize the training of deep networks.

Network architecture has also played a key role in addressing these challenges. For example, the ResNet architecture introduces "residual links" which allow the gradient to "skip" some layers during back-propagation , making it possible to train networks with hundreds of layers.

Although deep neural networks have the ability to model incredibly complex functions and revolutionize fields such as computer vision, machine translation and text generation, training such networks remains a challenge, stimulating the research community to come up with innovative solutions and endless creativity.

One of the major driving forces behind the advancement of deep learning has been the exponential growth in the availability of data. However, training deep neural networks requires huge amounts of data to produce accurate models. This has led to a growing reliance on so-called "big data". While the availability of such datasets has propelled progress in some fields, it has also raised privacy and ethical issues, with concerns about the processing and use of personal data without proper consent.

Another fundamental aspect of deep learning is the need for computational power. As networks have increased in depth, it has become imperative to have access to advanced hardware. Graphics Processing Units (GPUs) and, more recently, Tensor Processing Units (TPUs) have become essential for training deep neural networks. The emergence of these platforms has prompted companies like NVIDIA and Google to develop hardware specifically for deep learning.

However, despite its successes, deep learning also has its limitations.

For example, deep models tend to be "black boxes," meaning that while they may produce accurate results, it's often not clear how they made certain decisions.

This poses problems in sectors such as medicine or finance, where decision transparency is crucial. As a result, model interpretability research is gaining ground, seeking to make neural model decisions understandable.

Finally, one of the most recent challenges concerns energy efficiency. Training large deep learning models can consume enormous amounts of energy, equivalent to the electricity consumption of entire homes for several days. This concern has prompted research into more energy-efficient methods and the creation of "lightweight" neural architectures that maintain high performance with lower resource consumption.

In conclusion, while deep learning has led to revolutionary breakthroughs in various fields of technology, it continues to evolve, with new challenges and opportunities regularly emerging, stimulating scientists to push the limits of current knowledge.

## The Convolutions Neural Networks (CNN)

The Convolutions Neural Networks (CNN) represent one of the fundamental pillars in the field of deep learning, especially when it comes to tasks related to imaging and computer vision. They are particularly powerful in recognizing patterns within images, being able to distinguish details ranging from low to high frequencies.

The heart of CNNs is the convolution operation. In simple terms, during a convolution, a small filter (or kernel ) runs over the image pixel by pixel and produces a feature map. This filter is capable of extracting specific characteristics, such as contours, colors, textures or any other relevant pattern. For example, in a facial recognition application, initial filters might look for lines or curves, while filters in later layers might identify more complex structures like eyes or noses.

A distinctive feature of CNNs is their way of handling information locally, focusing on small portions of the image at a time. This local nature and the ability to share weights across the layer makes them extremely computationally efficient, reducing the number of parameters to train compared to traditional neural networks.

CNNs also include pooling layers , which reduce the spatial size of feature maps while keeping the most salient information. These layers usually use operations such as max-pooling , where only the highest value of a region is kept, allowing networks to become invariant to small translations and distortions.

In the modern landscape, CNNs have become fundamental in many applications. For example, they have been used to recognize objects in real-time images. A famous example is the VGG architecture developed by the Visual Geometry Group at the University of Oxford, which achieved notable results in the ImageNet image recognition challenge . Google's too Inception is another CNN architecture that has achieved impressive performance in image classification tasks.

In addition to classification, CNNs also find application in semantic segmentation, where the goal is not only to identify objects within an image, but also to delineate their boundaries. In this regard, the U-Net architecture, initially proposed to segment medical images, has been shown to have broad applicability in multiple segmentation domains.

The use of CNNs is not limited to images alone. For example, they have been adapted to work with timelines, three-dimensional data such as medical scans, and even video, demonstrating their versatility and ability to capture patterns in various data types.

Looking forward, as hardware evolves and datasets expand , CNNs are likely to become even more sophisticated, offering improvements in accuracy and the ability to capture ever more subtle and complex information.

With the increase in computational capabilities, especially thanks to the contribution of graphics processing units (GPU), the training and implementation of deep neural networks such as CNNs have become significantly more efficient. This has allowed scientists and researchers to experiment with even deeper and more complex architectures.

One of the interesting developments in the CNN domain is the adoption of Residual Networks ( ResNet ). Devised by researchers at Microsoft, these networks introduce the idea of "junk links" that bypass one or more layers. The magic behind ResNet lies in its design: rather than looking for a direct solution, the network looks for a residual solution. This means that ResNet learns the differences (or residuals) between the input and the desired output, simplifying the training process and helping to mitigate the gradient disappearance problem in deep architectures. This innovation has allowed networks to become much deeper, with some variants of ResNet boasting hundreds of layers.

Another significant advance is DenseNet , which further improves on the deep connect idea. Instead of bypassing only a few layers as in ResNet , in DenseNet each layer receives input from all previous layers. This dense connectivity showed higher metric efficiency and faster convergence during training.

The expansion of CNNs has also led to text-in-image recognition, as demonstrated by the successes of models such as CRNN, which combine CNNs for feature extraction with RNNs for sequential text decoding. This has proved particularly useful in applications such as recognizing car license plates or reading texts in natural environments.

Another area where CNNs have shown their potential is image synthesis and generative art. Variational Autoencoders (VAE) and Generative Adversarial Networks (GAN) utilize CNNs in both the generation and discrimination processes, allowing for the creation of high quality images that are often indistinguishable from the real thing .

In the modern business context, CNNs are now an essential component in video surveillance systems, where they can recognize and track people or vehicles, in medicine for the diagnosis of diseases through medical images, in autonomous vehicles for the perception of the surrounding environment and in many other applications.

As we move into the future, with the emergence of new computational paradigms such as edge computing and specialized hardware for AI, we can expect CNNs to become even more pervasive and powerful, enabling applications that might seem like science fiction today .

## Recurrent neural networks (RNN) and LSTM

Recurrent Neural Networks (RNN) represent a category of neural networks that are particularly effective in dealing with sequences of data, such as time series, text, audio signals and trajectories. Their peculiarity lies in the ability to "remember" information from previous inputs. This "remembering" occurs through cyclical connections within the network, allowing the information to persist.

Imagine reading a sentence or listening to a song. The understanding of a word or a note may depend on the previous ones. In an RNN, each element of a sequence is processed one at a time, taking into account not only the current input, but also some sort of "internal state" that captures information about previous inputs.

However, traditional RNNs face challenges in dealing with very long sequences. This is mainly due to the "disappearing gradient" problem, where the importance of information fades or disappears completely as the sequence gets longer. This is where an ingenious solution comes into play: LSTM, or Long Short- Term Memory.

LSTMs are a special variant of RNNs, designed to address the limitations of traditional RNNs. Their design includes what's called a "memory cell," which can hold information for long periods. An LSTM cell is made up of several "gates": the input gate, which decides which information to update; the forget gate, which decides what information to discard, and the exit gate, which decides what information will be used in the output. These gates work together to regulate the flow of information through the cell, ensuring that only relevant information persists over time.

In recent years, LSTMs have found application in many sectors. One of the most impressive examples is machine translation. Systems like Google Translate use LSTM-based architectures to translate text from one language to another in real time, taking into account the context of words and sentences. LSTMs have also been used in sentiment analysis, where the goal is to infer the emotion or sentiment of a text, and in text generation, where LSTMs can produce coherent narratives based on given styles and themes.

The audio field has also benefited from LSTM. For example, in speech recognition applications, LSTMs have been adopted to improve the accuracy of converting speech into text, considering the peculiarities and nuances of spoken language.

While RNNs and LSTMs have revolutionized many aspects of sequence processing, research continues to refine these techniques and discover new ways to capture and represent the complexities of sequential data. As hardware and optimization techniques evolve, we can expect the potential of recurrent neural networks to continue to blossom in ever more innovative ways.

Recurrent neural networks and, in particular, LSTMs have laid the groundwork for the development of other advanced architectures, some of which have been designed to address specific challenges associated with RNNs. One such challenge is the way RNNs handle information: while LSTMs were designed to deal with long-running sequences, there are certain situations where it is necessary to consider information from both the past and the future of a specific point in time. a sequence. From here emerges the idea of the Bidirectional RNN (BRNN).

BRNNs combine two RNNs into a single architecture: one RNN processes the sequence from top to bottom, while the other processes it from bottom to top. This allows the network to have information from both the past and the future when processing a specific point in the sequence. This bidirectional structure has proven particularly useful in speech recognition and image segmentation, where contextual information from both directions can offer meaningful insights.

Another notable advance in the field of recurrent neural networks has been the introduction of GRUs ( Gated Recurrent Units ). GRUs, like LSTMs, have been designed to address the problem of gradient disappearance in traditional RNNs. However, unlike LSTMs, GRUs use a more simplified structure with fewer gates, making them computationally lighter and, in some cases, offering similar or even better performance than LSTMs.

In modern contexts, recurrent neural networks have assumed a central role in applications such as chatbots and virtual assistants. Apple's Siri, for example, uses algorithms based on RNN and LSTM to understand and generate voice responses in real time. In the medical field, RNNs have been used to analyze time series of patient data, such as heartbeats and brainwaves, to predict potential abnormalities or seizures.

The field of music and art has also seen the emergence of RNN-based applications. Google's Magenta, a project exploring music and art creation through machine learning, has used RNN to generate new music and art styles.

While recurrent neural networks have already achieved remarkable milestones, the field is constantly evolving. As new algorithms emerge, existing architectures are optimized, and computational capabilities expand, RNNs and their variants can be expected to continue to be at the heart of the next wave of AI innovations.

## Modern applications of Deep Learning

Modern applications of deep learning are extraordinarily vast and are having a significant impact across industries, transforming our understanding of complex problems and revolutionizing the way challenges are approached. For example, in healthcare, convolutional neural networks (CNNs) are used to analyze medical images with a previously unattainable level of accuracy. CNN can detect abnormalities in X-rays, CT scans, and MRI scans with high accuracy, surpassing even human judgment in some cases.

multiclass classification to identify and locate diseases. Furthermore, in the field of natural language processing, or NLP, recurrent neural networks (RNNs) and Transformer Networks are particularly effective in dealing with the complex structure and sequentiality of language.

These advances have led to advances in machine translation, text generation, and sentiment analysis .

Algorithms like BERT and GPT-3, for example, are capable of performing tasks ranging from answering questions to creating text that is nearly indistinguishable from that written by a human.

In the realm of autonomous vehicles, deep learning is the backbone of perception and decision technologies.

Neural networks like YOLO ( You Only Look Once) and SSD (Single Shot Multibox Detector) are used for object recognition in real time. These networks are trained to identify and track various objects such as vehicles, pedestrians and road signs, allowing the car to navigate safely. To solve problems such as gradient disappearance, which afflicts neural models with many layers, techniques such as "Batch Normalization " and " Residual Networks" have been introduced. These techniques have paved the way for much deeper neural networks, increasing the model's ability to learn from large and complex data sets.

In the financial field, deep learning algorithms such as classification and regression neural networks have been implemented to predict the movement of stock prices, assess credit risk and detect fraud. Such models use a combination of structured and unstructured data to train the algorithm, making it highly accurate and reliable. Even the entertainment industry is using deep learning to generate realistic visual and audio effects. Software like DeepArt and DeepDream use neural networks to transform images and videos into specific artistic styles, while algorithms like WaveNet can generate realistic audio, like speech or music, from scratch.

retail and marketing industry , deep learning is used for product personalization and recommendation.

Algorithms such as matrix-based collaborative filtering systems use user behavior data to predict which products might be of interest to a particular customer. The high degree of personalization possible thanks to these algorithms has significantly improved the efficiency of advertising targeting , making online advertising more relevant and less invasive. In summary, deep learning is permeating every aspect of our lives, making systems smarter, more efficient and, in many cases, more humane. Its applications are as vast as its potential, and we continue to scratch the surface of what is possible.

Deep learning is pushing the boundaries of the possible in numerous areas of science, technology and the everyday. For example, in medicine, it is not only limited to analyzing medical images, but goes further, assisting in the discovery of new drugs. The complexity of pharmaceutical molecules and the infinite combinations of chemical compounds make the design of new drugs a monumental challenge. However, with the use of deep neural networks, the simulation and analysis of molecules becomes more feasible and accurate. Techniques such as reinforcement learning and generative models are used to discover new molecular structures that could be effective in treating specific diseases.

In the renewable energy space, deep learning helps optimize the efficiency of solar and wind power plants. For example, deep learning models can accurately predict weather variations that affect energy production, enabling more effective resource management. This becomes crucial when it comes to integrating renewable energy sources into a stabilized electricity grid.

In robotics, deep learning contributes to the refinement of algorithms that allow robots to interact with their environment in increasingly complex ways. For example, deep reinforcement learning, a combination of reinforcement learning and deep learning, has been used to train robots in tasks ranging from lifting objects to social interaction. Here, a robot can be trained to perform optimal actions through a system of rewards and punishments, improving with time and experience.

In journalism, deep learning is finding application in news tracking and analysis. Trained neural models can automatically categorize articles, identify fake news, and even generate summaries of complex events. Similarly, in the field of law, deep learning algorithms are being developed to assist in legal research, contract analysis, and prediction of legal process outcomes.

One of the most exciting frontiers is the brain-computer interface, where deep learning is used to decipher neural signals and translate them into commands for electronic devices. This has game-changing implications for people with disabilities, potentially offering new ways to communicate or control hearing aids.

In any case, it is important to note that with the enormous capabilities of deep learning also comes responsibility. Issues such as ethics, data privacy and the explainability of models are increasingly at the center of public and academic debate. New standards and regulations are being developed to ensure these technologies are implemented ethically and sustainably.

Hence, deep learning is not just a technical methodology; it is a driving force that is redeveloping entire industries and potentially the whole of society.

From healthcare to energy, from the law to education, its applications are countless and its potential benefits enormous, but as with any powerful technology, it's critical to handle it with care.

Deep learning is making great strides in the medical field, diagnosing diseases such as cancer with expert medical accuracy. Evolution in this area could lead to the direct integration of algorithms into medical imaging devices , providing real-time diagnosis. Personalized therapies could become the norm, with neural networks analyzing everything from genetic profiles to information from wearable devices like smartwatches .

In the renewable energy sector, deep learning is already optimizing the performance of wind turbines. In the future, we could see neural networks coordinating entire networks of renewable energy sources, adapting in real time to climate change and energy demand peaks. Robotics is another industry that benefits hugely from deep learning. Robots today can autonomously navigate unfamiliar and complex environments, and in the future we may have robotic assistants that understand and interpret human emotions, providing more natural and intuitive interaction.

Journalism and law are other industries where deep learning is starting to make an impact. Already today, algorithms can generate summaries of articles or analyze huge datasets to detect trends. In the future, journalists could collaborate with artificial intelligences to carry out detailed investigations in real time, while lawyers could use AI to analyze and predict the outcomes of legal cases.

Brain-computer interfaces, while still in their infancy, could radically change the way we interact with technology and with ourselves. Companies like Neuralink are trying to develop techniques to connect the human brain directly to computers, opening up possibilities such as controlling devices or even transferring thoughts and memories.

However, with this rapid evolution also come ethical and regulatory challenges. The explainability and verification of medical decisions made by algorithms will become crucial issues, as will the ethical implications of AI in areas such as surveillance and defence. With deep learning permeating so many aspects of our lives, it is essential to take these issues seriously to ensure the responsible and fair development of the technology.

# Chapter 5: Ethics and Bias in AI

In an age where artificial intelligence permeates every aspect of daily life, from smartphone apps to air traffic control systems, the question of ethics in AI has inevitably become central. Algorithms, once relegated to research labs and university classrooms, now make decisions that directly affect people's lives. They can decide who gets a loan, what medical treatment is most appropriate for a patient, or even whether a person is suspected of a crime. As a result, we are no longer just talking about technical or engineering matters; we are facing moral and ethical dilemmas that touch the heart of our social and individual values.

The ethical implications of AI are not a marginal subset of technological progress; they are a crucial component that forms the very soul of this revolution. To ignore ethics in AI is to risk creating systems that perpetuate inequalities, discriminate and, in the worst case, cause direct harm to human beings. However, taking ethics in AI seriously is not just a matter of avoiding negative outcomes; it is also a matter of actively directing the development of AI so that it brings the greatest benefit to society as a whole.

That is why this chapter is committed to exploring the importance of ethics in artificial intelligence. We will venture through various application areas, examine the most pressing ethical issues and discuss the laws and regulations that seek to address them. Our goal is to provide a comprehensive framework that helps not only developers and researchers, but also policy makers and the general public navigate the complicated ethical landscape of AI.

The importance of ethics in AI is multidimensional and touches on both technological and social aspects.

Ignoring ethical issues can lead to negative consequences not only for the individuals directly concerned, but for society as a whole. Ethics in artificial intelligence is of crucial importance for multiple reasons, each of which opens up a universe of considerations that go far beyond the mere fulfillment of laws and regulations.

Artificial intelligence has penetrated numerous sectors that directly affect human life and collective well-being. We talk about health, education, safety, jobs and transport, just to name a few. In the medical field, for example, machine learning algorithms are making diagnostic decisions and suggesting treatment plans. But what if an algorithm, due to a bias in the training data, recommended less effective treatments for certain sections of the population? Or if in the security sector, facial recognition algorithms were used in a discriminatory or inaccurate way, potentially unfairly limiting individual freedom? Such scenarios make it clear that algorithms are not just neutral tools; they act within social, ethical and political contexts.

AI bias is an insidious problem that touches many aspects of the design and implementation of AI technologies . Starting with data collection, it is important to recognize that datasets often reflect existing inequalities in society. For example, if we are building a speech recognition algorithm and we use a dataset composed mostly of native speakers of a language, the algorithm will be prone to making mistakes when it encounters different accents or dialects. This kind of bias built into the data can have real-world implications; in the case of speech recognition, it could result in poor accessibility of the service for people of different linguistic origins.

The problem also extends to the training phase of the algorithms. Algorithms learn from the data they are trained with, and if that data is infused with cultural, gender, or ethnic biases, the algorithm will inherit those biases. For example, in 2015, an algorithm used in the United States to predict a criminal's likelihood of reoffending was found to be heavily biased against African Americans. The algorithm was not inherently "racist", but had learned from historical data that, due to various social and institutional factors, they were heavily influenced by racial bias.

Even more alarming is when the bias is built into the algorithm design itself. This can happen when engineers make design choices that, while not intentionally discriminatory, have the effect of reinforcing certain stereotypes or inequalities. A famous example is that of the recommendation algorithms, used in platforms such as YouTube or Netflix , which are designed to maximize user engagement. This can lead to the creation of 'echo chambers' which reinforce already existing opinions, contributing to the polarization and spread of false or misleading information.

Given the complexity and pervasiveness of the problem, addressing bias in AI is a daunting task that requires coordinated action from several disciplines. From a technical point of view, we are working on more "fair" algorithms that can detect and correct the bias during the training phase. In parallel, the transparency and auditability of algorithms as control mechanisms is also being promoted. Furthermore, the education and awareness of engineers and decision -makers on the ethical risks associated with the use of AI is essential, to prevent human biases from being translated into algorithmic biases.

AI can exacerbate existing inequalities or create new ones. For example, AI systems in the credit sector could reinforce economic inequalities by denying loans to individuals from disadvantaged backgrounds due to metrics that may not reflect their real creditworthiness. Or, in education, using AI to personalize curricula could in theory improve teaching effectiveness, but also further marginalize students who lack access to these advanced technologies.

Artificial intelligence introduces new types of risks and vulnerabilities, such as the possibility of malicious or even destructive uses of technology. I am thinking, for example, of the use of AI-armed drones in war scenarios, or the abuse of algorithms for manipulating human behavior for political or commercial purposes. The ethical dimension therefore becomes fundamental for evaluating not only the current uses of technology, but also its possible future developments. AI thus raises fundamental questions about ethical action as such. In a world increasingly dominated by algorithms, what does it mean to be morally responsible? Is responsibility shared between developers, users, and perhaps even the algorithms themselves? This represents a new domain of ethical questioning, with profound implications for moral philosophy, law and society.

In this complex context, it is imperative to consider ethics as intrinsic and inextricable from the development and implementation of AI. Active attention to ethical issues is essential to guide the development of algorithms and systems that maximize human and social well-being while minimizing risk and discrimination.

AI can profoundly affect human identity and our understanding of ourselves. If algorithms can perform functions we once believed unique to humans, such as creativity or empathy, then we need to reevaluate what it means to be human. The question of the "simulated person" in AI, for example, raises complex ethical questions about consent, identity and the right to be forgotten.

The massive collection of data to power machine learning algorithms raises questions about who owns that data and how it is used. Irresponsible use of sensitive data can not only violate individual privacy, but also endanger groups of individuals, especially those who are already vulnerable. This could have implications in the context of public health, civil liberties and even national sovereignty.

The concept of 'autonomy', fundamental in ethics, is becoming increasingly relevant as AI advances. Increasingly intelligent algorithms are able to make decisions autonomously, without human intervention. How can we ensure that such decisions reflect human ethical values? Who is responsible when a self-driving car is involved in an accident?

AI technologies are developed and implemented in a variety of cultural, political and economic contexts. How can we ensure that algorithms are ethically sensitive to different populations and do not contribute to the dissemination of a certain set of cultural values at the expense of others?

This is particularly relevant when we consider the global diffusion of technologies such as surveillance systems. Finally, there is a growing consensus that AI ethics should not just be a posthumous consideration, but should be integrated into the entire lifecycle of developing and implementing technologies.

This ranges from ethics training for engineers and data scientists , to involving ethics committees in approving new projects, to setting up 'ethical audits' for algorithms already in use.

The importance of ethics in AI is, therefore, multifaceted and profound, crossing numerous domains ranging from the individual to society, from the local to the global. In a world where AI is destined to play an ever more pervasive role, attention to its ethical aspects is not just a matter of common sense, but an overriding necessity for the good of all.

The use of artificial intelligence in the past is a rapidly evolving field that has raised a number of ethical questions. A relevant case concerns the use of facial recognition algorithms by law enforcement and surveillance agencies. These apps have raised concerns about individual privacy and civil rights, particularly as they have often been used in a way that discriminates against certain communities or ethnic groups.

Ethics and morality are concepts historically reserved for humans, given our unique ability to reason, make informed choices, and possess a sense of responsibility. With the advancement of technology, especially in the field of artificial intelligence, these concepts are becoming more and more pertinent to the machine world as well. AI algorithms now make choices that can significantly impact people's lives, from medical decisions to credit ratings, and thus bring with them a new layer of ethical complexity.

One of the fundamental questions is whether ethics can be "codified". In other words, is it possible to program an algorithm to make ethical decisions? This opens a Pandora's box of what actually constitutes an "ethical" decision. Different individuals, cultures and societies have varying degrees of morality and ethical principles.

For example, while some may view the use of AI in facial recognition for national security as ethically acceptable, others may view it as an invasion of individual privacy.

Another critical aspect is transparency and "accountability ". With AI making increasingly complex decisions, it's difficult for humans to understand how these decisions are made. This raises ethical concerns about who should be held accountable in the event of errors or negative consequences. If a diagnostic algorithm suggests incorrect treatment leading to complications for the patient, who is to blame? The algorithm, the developers, or the doctors who trusted the algorithm?

The question of "algorithmic justice" is another theme that is emerging. The concern is that algorithms, if not carefully designed, can perpetuate and even exacerbate social inequalities. For example, if a risk assessment algorithm is trained on a dataset that contains racial or gender biases, the algorithm could in turn inherit these biases, leading to unfair decisions. Ethics in AI is not just a matter of programming morality into machines, but also how humans use this technology. The temptation to use AI for unethical purposes is always present. For example, AI could be used to develop autonomous weapons, raising ethical questions about who makes the final decision on the use of lethal force. As technology continues to evolve at an unprecedented rate, the need to address the complex ethical issues that arise becomes ever more urgent. This requires a multidisciplinary dialogue involving not only computer scientists and engineers, but also philosophers, ethicists , legislators and the general public.

The implication of the concepts of ethics and morality in the context of artificial intelligence is a critical discussion that takes on many facets. As AI technology creeps deeper and deeper into our daily lives, the urgency to look into these issues becomes ever more acute. Understanding how ethical principles apply to AI is a two-way process: not only do we need to consider how ethics fit into technology, but also how technology itself can influence and even shape our concepts of ethics and morality.

Traditional discourse on ethics has historically been anthropocentric, centered on the actions and decisions of human beings. However, with the advent of ever more sophisticated AI systems, these machines are taking on roles that were once the exclusive domain of humans. So the first question that arises is whether ethics, a field so closely related to human experience, can be applied to non-human entities.

This question becomes even more pertinent when these machines make decisions that directly impact human life, as is the case with the algorithms used in medicine to diagnose diseases or suggest treatments.

Another fundamental question is the universality or relativity of ethics in a world where AI is global. Different cultural contexts have different ethical norms and this can become problematic when trying to standardize ethical principles for AI systems that will be used internationally. For example, what is considered an invasion of privacy in one culture may not be perceived as such in another. A surveillance algorithm that is accepted in one country could be a cause for major ethical concern in another.

One of the more intricate issues is the transparency and interpretability of AI algorithms. Machine learning algorithms, in particular, can become "black boxes" that make it extremely difficult for humans to understand how certain decisions were made. This raises significant ethical issues, especially when errors occur. In a medical setting, for example, if a diagnostic algorithm makes a mistake that leads to ineffective treatment, the lack of transparency in the algorithm can severely hamper accountability and recurrence .

Furthermore, there is the critical issue of algorithmic justice. The data used to train the algorithms may contain implicit biases which, if not carefully evaluated and corrected, could be incorporated into the algorithm itself. This can have devastating effects in areas such as the justice system, where risk assessment algorithms could perpetuate or worsen already existing social inequalities.

Finally, there is the question of how AI itself might affect our concepts of ethics and morality. Technology has always impacted society and culture, and AI is no exception. It could challenge our traditional notions of autonomy, freedom and even conscience, leading to the reformulation of some of our most fundamental ethical principles.

So as AI continues to permeate every aspect of our lives, it's imperative that we carefully consider the ethical issues it brings with it. It is a task that requires an interdisciplinary approach, involving not only technologists, but also philosophers, sociologists, legislators and the public. Only through a thorough and honest examination of ethical issues can we hope to integrate AI into society in a way that maximizes benefits and minimizes harms.

In the field of artificial intelligence, the debate on ethics is a question that often splits into two distinct but interconnected directions: machine ethics and human ethics. While both avenues explore morality and responsibility, there is a crucial difference in their scope. Machine ethics are concerned with the moral principles that govern the behavior of algorithms and AI systems, while human ethics are concerned with the human decisions that are made in the design, implementation and use of these technologies.

In examining machine ethics, the discussion focuses on the rules and criteria that should guide the behavior of an AI system. The question arises as to whether a machine can be 'ethical' in the traditional sense of the word. Obviously, machines have no conscience, no emotions, or the ability to conduct moral reasoning. However, algorithms can be designed to follow certain ethical principles. For example, an autonomous vehicle could be programmed to minimize human harm in the event of an unavoidable crash. This type of programmatic decision can be seen as an extension of our understanding of ethics, adapted to the mechanical and algorithmic domain.

On the other hand, human ethics in AI deals with the responsibilities and moral decisions made by the humans who create and use these systems. For example, if a diagnostic algorithm in the medical field produces an error leading to ineffective treatment, the ethical question is not only whether the algorithm followed ethical principles in its design, but also whether the humans who created it acted in an ethical way.

Have they considered all possible outcomes? Have they tested the algorithm adequately? And most importantly, who is responsible when things go wrong?

While machine ethics can be viewed as a sub-field of applied ethics, the question of human ethics in the context of AI is broader and more complex. It goes to the heart of what it means to be human in an age where machines are taking on ever more complex and meaningful roles. This requires a redefinition of our traditional concepts of responsibility, guilt and merit in a context where decisions can be made or influenced by non-human entities.

Indeed, the distinction between machine ethics and human ethics is often more theoretical than practical, since the two are inextricably linked. The ethical decisions made during the design phase of an algorithm directly affect the ethical behavior of the machine. Similarly, the way a machine 'acts' can have a direct impact on the ethical decisions of humans who interact with it.

The interconnection between machine ethics and human ethics signals the need for a holistic approach to ethics in artificial intelligence. It is not enough just to program ethical principles into our machines; we also need to critically examine our own ethical standards and moral values in the context of AI. The goal should not only be to create machines that act ethically, but also to develop a deeper and more matrix understanding of ethics in an increasingly technology-dominated world. And to do that, we need an open, multidisciplinary dialogue involving technologists, philosophers, sociologists and a variety of other voices to navigate these increasingly complex ethical waters.

In the fast-changing modern world, AI has achieved a ubiquitous presence ranging from simple applications such as voice assistants and search engines to more complex solutions such as medical diagnosis systems and autonomous tanks.

But with the growing ubiquity of this technology, complex ethical issues are also emerging, one of which is the discrimination and bias encoded in AI systems.

For example, imagine a hiring algorithm that has been trained on historical data. If such data contains implicit biases regarding gender, ethnicity, or social class, the algorithm can perpetuate those biases, resulting in a form of systematic discrimination. One well-documented case is that of crime prediction algorithms, which have often exhibited racial bias due to the historical data they were trained on.

Not only can such systems perpetuate discrimination, they can also amplify it. Let's consider the recommendation algorithms used by social media that aim to keep the user engaged by showing content they might find interesting. If a user interacts with content that has a certain bias, the algorithm can interpret this as a preference and continue to show similar content, thereby reinforcing prejudicial beliefs and creating echo chambers.

The issue of discrimination and bias in AI extends far beyond algorithms and also touches on data representation. Take for example facial recognition applications. If an algorithm is trained primarily on images of individuals belonging to a particular ethnic group, it can perform poorly on individuals of other ethnic groups, resulting in inaccuracies that can have serious implications, for example in surveillance or security settings.

Solving this problem is not simple and requires a multi-dimensional approach that includes a critical examination of the data lifecycle, from acquisition to retention and use, as well as an ethical verification of the goal of the algorithm itself. It is crucial to include a diversity of voices in the decision-making process, to avoid unintentional bias.

AI developers need to be explicitly trained on ethics and discrimination issues, just as they are on security and privacy issues.

Measures to test, monitor and audit AI systems for bias should also be in place . Some modern initiatives such as ethical AI and humanistic technology seek to address these issues through an interdisciplinary approach, combining technical expertise with wisdom from fields such as philosophy, sociology and gender studies.

AI offers enormous opportunities for advancement and improvement in numerous sectors, it is imperative to seriously and rigorously address the issues of discrimination and prejudice that may arise. Ignoring these issues not only undermines social justice, it also undermines the effectiveness and usefulness of AI itself. As a society, we have an ethical responsibility to ensure these powerful technologies are developed and used in ways that maximize good while minimizing harm.

Tackling issues of discrimination and bias in the field of artificial intelligence requires a holistic and multidisciplinary approach, which goes far beyond the mere correction of algorithms. First, we need to look at the initial stages of the AI lifecycle – data collection. A more ethically thoughtful and balanced collection of data can prevent many root problems.

For example, in the case of facial recognition, making sure your dataset is representative of different ethnicities, genders, and social groups can avoid many false positives or negatives.

Furthermore, the design of the algorithm itself should be informed by a sound understanding of the ethical and social implications of the technology. This could involve working with experts in ethics, sociology and law to ensure that ethical considerations are incorporated from the outset.

But even the best forward planning isn't enough. It is crucial to have auditing and evaluation procedures in place to monitor how these systems perform in the real world. This could include external audits by third-party organizations that evaluate an algorithm's ethical impact, not just its technical accuracy.

Rigorous scrutiny can reveal biases and discriminations that weren't immediately apparent during the development stage.

A growing solution is the use of "explainable AI," which focuses on machine learning models that can make their decisions transparent. Having a clear picture of how the algorithm works can help identify and correct biases. However, it is important to note that simple transparency is not a panacea and must be coupled with other measures to be effective. Another important consideration is the social responsibility of companies that develop and distribute AI-based technologies. A robust corporate code of ethics and a culture that prioritizes fairness can go a long way in mitigating problems before they become large-scale. Some companies are already implementing roles like " Ethical AI Practitioner " or " Chief Ethics Officer " to oversee these aspects. Finally, the importance of training cannot be underestimated. Engineers and data scientists must be educated not only in the technical disciplines, but also in the ethical principles that guide the responsible use of technology. Courses in ethics AI and bias and discrimination training should be an integral part of computer science and engineering education.

Therefore the issue of discrimination and bias in AI is complex and there is no one-size-fits-all solution. However, with a holistic approach involving various stakeholders and discipline, significant steps can be taken towards creating fairer and more equitable AI systems.

The relationship between artificial intelligence and privacy is a delicate dance that embodies one of the fundamental tensions of our time: that between technological progress and the protection of human rights. While technology offers us an extraordinary range of services and conveniences, it often requires a certain amount of personal data in return. In this symbiotic relationship, AI plays a double role: it is both a catalyst for the problem and part of the solution.

Think of the smart devices that inhabit our homes, such as voice assistants, smart thermostats and security bells. These devices collect an impressive amount of data, often of a very personal nature. Once this data is collected and sent to corporate servers, it becomes susceptible to being analyzed by AI algorithms for a wide variety of purposes: targeted advertising, behavioral analysis, and even state surveillance. Here, the question of privacy takes on a new urgency. Who controls this data? How are they used, and who has access to them? Another illuminating example is the growing ubiquity of facial recognition systems. This technology, powered by deep learning algorithms, has the potential to erode our privacy in ways that were unthinkable just a decade ago. Going unnoticed in a crowd becomes nearly impossible when every surveillance camera is potentially an identification device. The threat also extends to freedom of expression and association, as individuals may be discouraged from attending rallies or other public events for fear of being misidentified or followed.

But AI isn't just a problem; it can also be part of the solution. For example, AI-powered encryption algorithms offer new ways to protect personal data. AI can also be used to detect suspicious activity or data breaches in real time, providing an extra layer of security. The big picture here is that while AI presents clear privacy challenges, it also offers new avenues for data protection. The key is to strike a balance, one that will require thoughtful regulation, ethical design and continued vigilance from all stakeholders involved. This is not only a technical but a profoundly ethical challenge, forcing us to balance the tangible benefits of AI with its potential for unprecedented intrusion into our private lives.

The topic of privacy and surveillance in the age of artificial intelligence also extends to the corporate world and the research arena. Companies, for example, are increasingly using AI algorithms to analyze the behavior of their employees.

These tools may monitor efficiency, but they also raise serious questions about the right to privacy in the workplace. Where do we draw the line between legitimate work efficiency monitoring and invasive surveillance that can negatively affect employee morale?

In addressing AI-related privacy and surveillance issues, companies are adopting a variety of techniques and technologies. Encryption, for example, is a common method of protecting sensitive data. Advanced forms of encryption, such as encrypted data processing, allow an algorithm to perform calculations on the data without having to decrypt it , providing an extra layer of security.

Data minimization is another important strategy. Here, the idea is to collect only the data that is strictly necessary to perform a specific operation. This reduces the risk of data exposure and unauthorized use. Similarly, some companies are exploring the use of synthetic data – information that has been generated by an algorithm to replicate statistics from a real dataset, but which cannot be traced back to real individuals. Another emerging approach is the use of Federated Learning techniques. In this model, a machine learning algorithm is trained on multiple devices or decentralized servers, without ever transferring data off those devices. This allows you to leverage data from a variety of sources without compromising user privacy.

The use of "Privacy- Preserving AI" is also gaining traction. This is a branch of information science that focuses on methods for training and implementing AI models in such a way as to minimize the disclosure of sensitive information.

Techniques such as " differential privacy" offer mathematical guarantees that individuals' information will not be revealed during data analysis. In addition to technological techniques, companies are also implementing internal policies and governance mechanisms to address these issues.

Internal ethics committees, often composed of a variety of stakeholders that include ethicists , jurists, and technologists, are becoming more common. These committees can conduct ethical impact assessments, review design decisions, and provide guidance on issues such as data collection, consent, and transparency.

Companies are also looking to engage consumers and end users in the privacy discussion. Tools such as privacy dashboards that allow users to see exactly what data is being collected and how it is being used, as well as to withdraw consent if necessary, are becoming more common. While the challenge of balancing the capabilities of AI with respect for privacy and individual freedom is great, multi-pronged efforts are underway to address this issue. Through a combination of technological advancements, corporate governance, and stakeholder engagement, companies are seeking to build an AI ecosystem that is not only powerful, but also ethical and respectful of individual rights.

Even in the research field, AI algorithms are used to analyze huge datasets that can include sensitive information. For example, medical research might use patient data to develop new treatments and therapies. While these initiatives may have a positive impact on public health, it is crucial to ensure data is anonymised and adequately protected to prevent abuse. It should be noted that the concept of "anonymity" is becoming increasingly difficult to maintain as data mining techniques advance . Advanced algorithms can sometimes "de-anonymize" data, linking information that seemingly had no personal identifier to specific individuals. This raises further ethical questions about data collection and use, even when the intentions may be benevolent.

Another significant dimension is the intersection between AI and mass surveillance. States can use AI to monitor citizens' communications and activities on a scale never seen before.

While these capabilities could be used for legitimate purposes such as crime prevention or national defense, there is also a risk that they may be used in ethically questionable ways, such as to stifle protests or to discriminate against certain communities.

So how can all these concerns be addressed? Regulation is a key tool, and we have seen initiatives in different parts of the world in this regard. The European Union's General Data Protection Regulation (GDPR) is an example of how the law can try to balance the opportunities offered by AI technology with citizens' right to privacy. Ethical impact assessments, responsible design guidelines and reporting mechanisms are other avenues that can be followed to ensure the ethical use of AI. The issue of privacy and surveillance in AI is a complex knot that harnesses technology, ethics, law and society together. Tackling this knot will require a concerted effort from all stakeholders, from technologists to lawmakers, activists to ordinary citizens. Only through open dialogue and a commitment to shared responsibility can we hope to successfully navigate the tumultuous waters that this new age of technology has opened before us.

## Health care

The ethical implications of using AI in medicine are numerous and complex, touching on areas such as diagnostics, treatments and patient data management. Let's start with the diagnostics. AI has the ability to analyze large amounts of medical data in a very short time, allowing doctors to identify conditions and diseases with unprecedented accuracy. However, this ability raises ethical questions, such as liability for misdiagnosis. If an algorithm fails, who is responsible? The doctor, the software developer, or both?

In the context of medical diagnostics, artificial intelligence has ushered in a new era in which machines can analyze complex data such as radiological images, genetic test results, and even electrical signals from the heart with a precision that, in some cases, surpasses that of human experts. This opens up enormous potential to improve the speed and accuracy of diagnoses, which in turn can lead to more timely and effective treatments. However, the use of AI-based diagnostic algorithms raises important ethical questions.

One of the most obvious dilemmas is liability in the event of an error. If an algorithm, for whatever reason, generates a misdiagnosis that leads to mistreatment, who is to blame? It's a complex issue that touches the entire chain of responsibility, from the creators of the algorithm, to the data providers it was trained on, to the doctors using AI as a diagnostic tool. This uncertainty can lead to a legal and ethical gray area that could hinder the adoption of these technologies if not addressed properly. Also, there's the issue of accessibility. Advanced algorithms are often developed by large technology companies or research institutions with significant financial resources. If access to such diagnostic tools becomes expensive or limited to certain healthcare settings, a form of inequality of care could emerge. In other words, only those who can afford access to these advanced technologies could benefit from the more precise diagnoses, leaving others having to rely on more traditional and potentially less effective methods.

Another critical aspect is that of equity in the quality of diagnoses. If an algorithm is trained on a dataset that is primarily composed of individuals of a certain ethnicity, gender, or socioeconomic group, there is a risk that diagnoses for individuals outside that group will not be accurate.

This form of bias could not only perpetuate existing inequalities in the health care system, but could also lead to serious misdiagnoses for unrepresented populations.

The transparency and understandability of algorithms is another area of ethical concern.

Many of these machine learning techniques are considered "black boxes," meaning that while we can see what goes in and what goes out, the internal decision-making process is murky even to experts. This poses an ethical problem, especially when an algorithm suggests a diagnosis or treatment that goes against medical intuition or standard guidelines. The use of AI in diagnostics offers tremendous opportunities but also introduces a number of ethical dilemmas that require careful scrutiny and thoughtful regulation. Multidisciplinary collaboration between technology, legal, medical and ethical professionals is essential to address these issues fairly and responsibly.

Diagnostic algorithms may not be equally effective for all populations, as many algorithms have been trained on data from specific demographic groups. This can lead to unintentional discrimination and lower quality of care for certain communities. It is therefore crucial to ensure that the data used to train these algorithms is representative and that the algorithms themselves are independently audited to ensure they do not discriminate against certain groups. As for medical treatments, AI holds the promise of more personalized and potentially more effective therapies. For example, algorithms could suggest specific treatment protocols based on a patient's genetic profile. However, this opens up an ethical debate on the privacy and ownership of genetic data. Who owns this information? What are the risks of genetic discrimination by insurers or employers?

When we talk about artificial intelligence-based medical treatments, we enter particularly sensitive territory, as the decisions made could have a direct impact on the life and death of patients.

AI has the potential to tailor treatments based on patient data, making them more effective and potentially reducing side effects. For example, in the field of oncology, algorithms can be used to predict how a particular tumor will react to various drugs or forms of radiation therapy, allowing doctors to optimize the treatment regimen for each individual patient. However, the involvement of AI in medical treatments raises several ethical questions that are even more complex than those in diagnostics. A crucial point is the autonomy of the patient. Conventional medical practice places particular emphasis on informed consent, where the patient must be fully aware of the potential risks and benefits of the suggested treatment. But with algorithms operating as "black boxes," how can a patient give truly informed consent? While not even experts can fully explain how an algorithm decides a given course of treatment, there is a clear conflict with the principle of patient autonomy.

Alongside this, there is the risk of overfitting, where an AI model becomes too specific for the data it was trained on. In a treatment setting, this could mean that the algorithm may not generalize well when applied to patients with different characteristics than those in the training set. This could lead to ineffective or, at worst, harmful treatments for certain patient populations. Also, as is the case with diagnostics, legal and medical liability in AI-based treatments is a gray area. If an AI-guided treatment were to fail or produce unexpected side effects, accountability could be difficult to establish. Is it the doctor who followed the recommendations of the algorithm? Is it the team of data scientists who trained the algorithm? Or is it the AI itself? These are questions that still have no definitive answers and represent a significant ethical obstacle.

Another ethical dilemma concerns the distribution of these technologies. AI in medical treatments could be a luxury that only the most advanced and well-funded healthcare systems can access. This limitation could amplify existing inequalities in the quality of health care globally. If the most effective and personalized treatments are available only in some places or for those who can afford them, an ethical disparity is created that goes beyond the simple question of technological availability.

AI has game-changing potential in improving the efficacy of medical treatments, it introduces an ethical complexity that cannot be ignored. Deep reflection on these ethical issues is imperative, and as with diagnostics, will require a collaborative effort across different sectors to address these dilemmas in a responsible and humane way.

In the context of patient data management, AI can provide advanced tools for organizing and analyzing health data, which could lead to better quality of care. However, the collection, storage and analysis of sensitive data pose huge privacy risks. Medical data is some of the most personal information a person can have, and its misuse or exposure can have serious consequences.

Patient management is another area where artificial intelligence is having a significant impact, and as in other areas of healthcare, the ethical implications are of paramount importance. For example, intelligent systems can be used to monitor the health status of patients in real time, sending alerts to doctors if conditions deteriorate. This constant monitoring capability offers the possibility of timely interventions, but also raises questions about how sensitive patient data is managed and protected.

The ethical question here also focuses on the issue of consent.

Many patients may not be aware of the level of surveillance they are undergoing or the complexity of the algorithms that analyze their data. In the worst case, these systems could also be used to profile patients, classifying them into categories that could influence the quality or speed of care they receive. For example, an algorithm might identify a patient as "low-risk" for certain complications, and thus his or her symptoms might be given less weight than those of another patient classified as "high-risk." This categorisation, if incorrect, could lead to suboptimal care and raise serious ethical questions. Another aspect of patient management is coordination of care. Intelligent algorithms can help doctors make more informed decisions about how to allocate resources such as hospital beds, staff and equipment. However, if these algorithms are trained on data that reflect existing biases in the healthcare system or society at large, they could perpetuate or worsen inequalities in access to care.

And let's not forget the human aspect of patient management. While AI can handle things like scheduling appointments or predicting a patient's needs, it can't (or at least shouldn't) replace the human touch, empathy, and moral judgment that are at the heart of medical practice. Overuse of algorithms in patient management could risk depersonalizing healthcare, making patients little more than numbers in a system.

AI-enabled patient management is an evolving practice, with multiple ethical facets that need careful thought.

Every advantage offered by technology must be balanced with ethical considerations that place the patient's well-being at the center of the decision-making process. The challenge is to integrate AI in a way that improves the efficiency and effectiveness of healthcare, without sacrificing fundamental ethical principles such as autonomy, justice and human dignity.

## Mobility and Security

The growing presence of autonomous cars on the roads represents one of the most interesting cases of how artificial intelligence is changing the dynamics of our daily lives. In addition to promising improvements in traffic efficiency and safety, these technologies open a Pandora's box of complex ethical issues facing society. One of the most discussed moral dilemmas in this context is the so-called "tram problem," a thinking exercise that confronts a vehicle with an impossible decision: who to save and who to sacrifice in an unavoidable emergency situation.

In a world where driving decisions are made by algorithms rather than humans, the "tram problem" becomes not just a hypothetical question but an engineering challenge. In a fraction of a second, the car's software will have to weigh variables such as passenger safety, pedestrian presence, road conditions and traffic laws to make a decision that could have fatal implications. This raises the question of who is really responsible in the event of an accident: is it the car, the programmer who wrote the algorithm, the manufacturer of the car, or even the regulatory body that allowed the car to be on the roads?

Another critical point is the concept of justice and impartiality in planning the decisions that autonomous cars will have to take. If, for example, an algorithm is programmed to minimize the total damage in the event of an accident, it could theoretically decide to sacrifice the passenger to save a group of pedestrians. But is it ethically acceptable to program a machine to make such a decision? And if so, who has the right to set these criteria?

The matter becomes even more complicated when we consider that these driving algorithms will likely be trained on huge datasets that include demographic, historical and behavioral information. There is a risk that existing biases in the data translate into discriminatory decisions by the AI. For example, if an algorithm is trained on traffic crash data that shows a higher crash rate in certain areas, it could develop driving strategies that avoid those areas, potentially perpetuating social stereotypes and economic inequalities.

And there is also the issue of transparency and accountability. The algorithms that drive these cars are extremely complex and often protected as trade secrets. This makes it difficult for the public, and even experts, to understand exactly how these ethically charged decisions are made. In a context as critical as road safety, it is imperative that there is some degree of transparency and accountability in how autonomous cars operate.

Self-driving cars offer enormous promise to improve our lives in many ways, they are not without a number of ethical challenges that require serious and thorough consideration.

As a society, we must engage in an open and inclusive dialogue to establish the ethical principles that will guide this revolutionary technology. Only then can we realize the benefits of autonomous cars without compromising the fundamental values of justice, equity and human dignity.

## Manipulation of Public Opinion

The manipulation of public opinion is a topic that acquires particular relevance in the age of artificial intelligence and big data.

While previously the tools available to influence opinion were mainly traditional media such as newspapers and television, today social media and online platforms offer powerful new means of shaping the thinking and behavior of the masses.

Artificial intelligence amplifies this capability in ways that were previously unthinkable, allowing for the segmentation and personalization of information on a massive scale.

Recommendation algorithms, for example, use data about past behavior to predict and influence future behavior. When applied ethically, this can improve the user experience by suggesting products or content that are truly relevant to the individual. However, when used unethically, it can also be used to reinforce existing prejudices, isolate individuals in information bubbles, and even propagate disinformation.

We must not underestimate the role of deepfakes , images or videos manipulated through advanced algorithms, which can create convincing but completely false scenarios. Deepfakes can be used to spread false narratives, jeopardizing trust in the information system and, ultimately, in democratic institutions . Politicians can be made to appear as if they have said or done things that are not true, causing unwarranted scandals or influencing the outcome of elections.

These manipulation techniques can have profound and long-lasting impacts on society. They can fuel polarization and extremism, eroding the social fabric and making civil dialogue increasingly difficult. Furthermore, they can have serious consequences on people's mental health, creating anxiety, stress and a feeling of helplessness in the face of an increasingly complex and deceptive world.

One of the burning questions is how to regulate the use of artificial intelligence in these manipulative activities. While heavy censorship is generally undesirable in a free and open society, there is growing consensus that some form of oversight is needed to prevent abuse. Transparency and accountability become key concepts: it is important that users are aware of the fact that they are interacting with algorithms and that they have the ability to understand how these machines make decisions that concern them.

The social media arena is particularly sensitive to the issue of manipulating public opinion, especially with global platforms such as Facebook , Twitter , Instagram and TikTok holding huge amounts of user data. The algorithms of these platforms are designed to maximize user interaction, often at the expense of the truthfulness or quality of the information presented.

Think, for example, of the 2016 US presidential election and Facebook- mediated foreign interference . Fake pages and accounts have spread misleading information, helping to further polarize an already divided electorate. Twitter has also been criticized for the ease with which fake or misleading news can go viral, amplified by both real users and bots.

Instagram and TikTok , while primarily photo and video sharing platforms, aren't immune to these problems. The trend towards aesthetic perfection and the presentation of an idealized lifestyle can create unrealistic expectations, negatively affecting the self-esteem and mental well-being of users, especially among the younger ones.

Platforms themselves have begun to take steps to tackle misinformation and abuse, such as fact-checking and labeling problematic content. However, these measures are often seen as insufficient or even contradictory. For example, labeling posts as "controversial" on Facebook has in some cases had the opposite effect, increasing the interest and circulation of the content in question.

These challenges pose urgent questions about who should have the power to regulate information in such a democratic and borderless space as the internet. It is a topic that involves not only the developers of technologies and the companies that use them, but also the legislators, the control bodies and, ultimately, the users themselves. The solution is not simple and requires a multipolar and multilayered approach that takes into account the complexity and global interconnectedness of social media platforms.

In general, while social media and artificial intelligence offer extraordinary possibilities for connection and access to information, they bring with them new and exponential ethical responsibilities. The choices we make today about how to govern and use these powerful technologies will shape the shape of our public discourse and the very fabric of our society for years to come.

Some of the most well-known examples of manipulating public opinion through the use of social platforms and artificial intelligence involve electoral campaigns and disinformation on sensitive topics such as health and safety.

During the 2016 US presidential election, foreign agents were widely documented to have used Facebook to spread disinformation. They created fake pages and groups pretending to represent American interests and used these to spread false or misleading news. The intent was to sow discord and polarization among voters. This case has drawn global attention to the potential of social media platforms to influence real events, to the point that even the US Congress has held hearings to look into the phenomenon.

The COVID-19 pandemic has created fertile ground for the spread of conspiracy theories and disinformation, thanks in part to the unprecedented nature of the crisis and people's susceptibility to information that confirms their pre-existing beliefs or fears. Many of these conspiracies have found fertile ground on social media, where algorithms designed to maximize user interaction can indirectly promote sensationalized or divisive content.

The theory that the virus was created in a laboratory and intentionally released has been widely spread despite lack of solid scientific basis. Not only does this theory divert attention from constructive discussions about how to handle the pandemic, it can also fuel xenophobic sentiments and endanger blamed ethnic communities.

Another notable example is misinformation regarding COVID-19 vaccines. Unsubstantiated theories have questioned both the efficacy and safety of vaccines, often citing misleading or anecdotal data.

This kind of misinformation not only breeds mistrust in the efficacy of vaccines, but can also lead to reduced vaccine coverage, jeopardizing efforts to achieve herd immunity and prolonging the duration of the pandemic.

Additionally, conspiracy theories regarding social distancing measures and the wearing of masks have helped polarize public opinion. In some cases, this has led to public outcry against lockdown measures, endangering both individuals and communities as a whole.

Social media platforms have been criticized for not doing enough to counter misinformation. While some have begun tagging or removing misleading content and directing users to trusted sources, these measures are often seen as insufficient. The issue is complex and raises ethical questions about how to balance freedom of expression with the need to protect public health.

In India, spreading false information via WhatsApp has led to serious consequences, including mob violence. For example, messages encouraging hatred and disinformation against minority ethnic or religious groups circulated, sometimes resulting in incidents of communal violence.

These examples highlight the seriousness of manipulating public opinion through social media and technology. They highlight the urgent need to address these issues at an ethical level, to better understand how technology can be designed and regulated to protect the integrity of public discourse and the well-being of society.

In short, artificial intelligence offers powerful tools that can be used both for good and for evil in manipulating public opinion.

The key to navigating this new landscape is a deep ethical commitment on the part of those developing and deploying these technologies, coupled with a robust regulatory framework that can provide safeguards against the most serious abuses.

The stakes are high: the cohesion of society and the functioning of democracy as we know it may depend on the decisions we make today about how to manage this powerful new form of influence.

## Responsibility or Accountability

The question of liability in case of errors committed by Artificial Intelligence systems is one of the most complex and discussed areas in the field of AI ethics. With the increase in the use of AI in critical sectors such as healthcare, transportation and security, the need to clarify who is responsible when things go wrong has become increasingly urgent.

One aspect that complicates the matter is the inherently complex and often " black box" nature of many AI algorithms. For example, deep neural networks are notorious for being difficult to interpret, making it difficult to determine exactly why a particular error occurred. This poses both technical and ethical challenges. If we can't fully understand how a decision was made, how can we know for sure who or what is responsible?

Another element that adds complexity is the involvement of multiple actors in the life cycle of an AI system. From designing and developing the model, to collecting and curating the data on which the model was trained, to implementing and using the system in a real-world context, each stage offers opportunities for errors and, therefore, potential liability.

It could be the team of data scientists who developed the algorithm, the organization that collected the data, the organization that implemented the system, or the end user who interacted with it in an unexpected way.

In healthcare, for example, an incorrect diagnostic algorithm could lead to ineffective or even harmful treatment. In this case, one could point the finger at the development team for not properly validating the algorithm, or at the medical staff for not exercising adequate clinical judgment. Again, liability may fall on the health care agency if the error is found to be due to inadequate or biased training data .

The matter is further complicated when it comes to autonomous AI systems, such as autonomous cars. If an autonomous vehicle is involved in an accident, it is difficult to determine whether the responsibility rests with the software, the vehicle manufacturer, the owner or other road actors involved. These scenarios raise legal and moral dilemmas, such as the famous "tram problem," which investigates how a machine should ethically "choose" in a situation where every available option entails some degree of harm.

Liability for errors committed by AI is, therefore, an area that requires careful consideration by lawyers, ethicists , technologists and regulators. Solutions such as independently auditing AI systems, building regulatory frameworks, and implementing ethical principles can provide some avenues for addressing these complex issues. However, it is clear that there is no simple or one-size-fits-all solution, and the debate over who is responsible for AI mistakes is likely to remain a central question in AI ethics for years to come.

Thus, it becomes essential to also consider the context of use and social expectations. For example, in high-stakes contexts such as healthcare or national security, tolerance for faults might be much lower than in less critical applications, such as recommendation engines. This leads to important questions about which standards of quality and reliability should be applied to different types of AI systems.

Another key aspect is the evolution of algorithms and data over time. Since AI is inherently a "learning" technology, what is considered a "mistake" may change as the system adapts and improves. This raises questions about the concept of temporal responsibility: is an error that occurred in the past always attributable to the same entities even if the system has been updated or changed?

Further complication arises from globalization. Very often, the data used to train the algorithms is collected from different parts of the world and the models are implemented across national borders. In this scenario, which laws and regulations are applicable? How can ethical and normative differences between different cultures and legal systems be resolved?

Given the complexity of the issue, several initiatives are emerging to address the liability issue in AI. For example, some suggest the use of "transparency cards" detailing how an algorithm works, what data it uses, and how the results have been validated. Others propose implementing " explainability systems " that can translate the algorithm's decisions into terms humans can understand, thus providing a basis for attributing accountability.

In the legal field, there is discussion about whether algorithms could be considered as legal "agents", thus allowing a sort of direct responsibility for the decisions taken. While controversial, this idea raises the important question of how laws and regulations should evolve to keep pace with technological innovations.

Liability for mistakes made by AI systems is a highly complex ethical and legal issue that challenges our traditional notions of guilt, intentionality and accountability. It requires a multidisciplinary approach that combines technical expertise with profound ethical and legal reflections.

It is not a question that can be solved by a single discipline or with simplistic solutions. As AI continues to permeate our society, the issue of accountability will be at the center of public and scientific debate, requiring concerted efforts to address the challenges that will inevitably emerge.

The expression "black box opening" in the context of artificial intelligence refers to the act of making the inner workings of an AI model understandable. Many machine learning algorithms, especially those employed in deep learning, are notoriously difficult to interpret. This is because, despite their effectiveness in making accurate predictions or performing specific tasks, the underlying logic that leads to such decisions is not immediately apparent, even to experts in the field. In practice, we know that they "work", but it is not always clear "how" or "why" they work.

This becomes a serious issue when we consider the ethical implications. For example, if an algorithm used for credit scoring denies an individual a loan, it is crucial to understand on what basis this decision was made. Was it unintentional discrimination based on factors such as ethnicity, gender or age? Or was the decision made on the basis of legitimate and objective criteria? Without a way to "open the black box," it's difficult, if not impossible, to judge the fairness or ethics of decisions made by an algorithm.

subdiscipline of AI research has grown that focuses on the interpretability and explainability of models. These works seek to develop new algorithms that are not only effective at their task, but also offer some form of comprehensible reasoning that can be examined by humans.

Some of these attempts go through techniques of " local interpretability ", which seek to explain individual decisions made by the model, while others aim for a "global interpretability ", i.e. an understanding of the algorithm as a whole.

In the legal and regulatory arena, the European Union with its General Data Protection Regulation (GDPR) has taken steps towards the need for explainability , establishing that individuals have the right to receive explanations about automated decisions that have a significant impact about their life. However, the practical realization of this principle remains an open challenge.

The opening of the black box is therefore not only a technical question but a profoundly ethical one. Having full access to AI decision-making is essential to ensure that technology is used in a way that respects the fundamental principles of justice, equity and human dignity. And, even more generally, to build public trust in these technologies, which are having an increasingly pervasive impact on our lives.

The future of the field of artificial intelligence promises developments that are both exciting and ethically problematic. As we expect technology to continue to evolve, improving medical diagnosis, the safety of autonomous cars and the efficiency of global distribution systems, new ethical dilemmas are equally likely to emerge that we can only guess at at present.

One area that could produce such problems is the growing integration of AI with human biology. The lines between humans and machines may become increasingly blurred with the adoption of brain-computer interfaces and other implantable devices.

These devices could enhance human capabilities in previously unimaginable ways, but they raise questions about who will have access to these technologies and how they might be used or abused.

New forms of inequality and discrimination based on biotechnological "improvement" could emerge, jeopardizing fundamental concepts of equity and human rights.

The potential for creating artificial general intelligence, a form of AI with general cognitive skills comparable to humans, also presents a minefield of ethical issues. An AI with the ability to determine itself, or even to feel emotions and desires, would raise troubling questions about the rights and duties of both humans and machines. And if these machines were able to subvert human controls, how would we ensure global safety and well-being?

In the geopolitical context, the use of AI for mass surveillance or automated warfare is another focal point. Some states could use AI to strengthen autocratic regimes, undermining the rights and freedoms of entire populations. Furthermore, the use of drones and other autonomous technologies in the military opens the door to new types of conflict, where the distinction between combatants and civilians may become even more blurred.

The issue of the environment is another often overlooked aspect. While AI has the potential to help combat climate change through resource optimization and environmental monitoring, the energy consumption of the infrastructure needed to support advanced AI models could have significant environmental impacts. What will be the net ecological balance of the use of AI?

The potential for manipulation on a global scale through social media platforms will continue to grow. With AI becoming ever more effective at understanding and influencing human behavior, the spread of fake news, conspiracy theories and hate speech could increase.

AI may have the potential to solve some of humanity's biggest problems, it is crucial that the fullest attention is paid to the ethical implications of this powerful technology. Ethical oversight and regulation will need to be constantly updated to keep pace with rapid advances in the field, ensuring that benefits are distributed fairly and risks are mitigated effectively.

Preparing society for the future challenges posed by artificial intelligence is a highly complex task that requires a multipolar approach. As technology advances at a rapid pace, public and private institutions, as well as individuals, must be proactive in setting an ethical path for its development and application. One of the main strategies is the creation of multidisciplinary ethics committees. These groups should include AI experts, ethicists , jurists, sociologists, and community representatives, among others. Their task would be to evaluate emerging applications of AI, proposing guidelines, standards and regulations that can guide technological development in an ethically sustainable direction. This approach has already been adopted by some organizations and has the potential to provide a solid basis for informed decisions.

In parallel, a strong investment in education and public awareness is needed. Many of the ethical challenges posed by AI are complex and contradictory, and an informed public is essential to navigating the inherent moral dilemmas. Educational programs on technology ethics, developer training, and information campaigns can help prepare society for the complex decisions that will inevitably have to be made. On the R&D front, encouragement to develop responsible AI is key. That means encouraging practices like ethical design from the start, independent auditing of AI systems, and transparency in how data is collected and used. A step in this direction could be the creation of tax incentives or grants for companies that adopt ethical practices in the use of AI.

In the legal arena, the law will have to evolve to keep pace with the new challenges posed by AI. This could include new data privacy laws, regulations on the use of AI in sensitive fields such as medicine or surveillance, and perhaps most controversially, the development of a legal framework that addresses the question of the "personality" of advanced artificial intelligences.

It is also imperative that an open and continuous dialogue is established on a global scale. The challenges posed by AI know no geographical boundaries and will require international collaboration to be effectively addressed. International organisations, governments and multinational companies have an important role to play in facilitating these exchanges and in ensuring that ethical standards are shared and enforced on a global scale.

In the age of rapid technological evolution, artificial intelligence has proven itself as a revolutionary force with the potential to improve many aspects of human life. However, this potency comes with its own set of ethical challenges that cannot be overlooked. Ethical issues span a wide range of areas, from healthcare and discrimination to the manipulation of public opinion and legal liability. In the medical field, AI can contribute enormously to diagnosis and treatment, but it also raises ethical questions regarding transparency, accuracy and patient privacy. Similarly, the power of AI to analyze huge datasets can also be used to discriminate, both intentionally and unintentionally.

Lack of transparency into how these decisions are made by opaque algorithms can undermine public trust and hinder accountability. In the context of social media, AI can be exploited to spread disinformation, thereby influencing public opinion on critically important issues such as elections or public health. Regarding accountability, the field is still evolving on how to attribute blame or intent when an AI system makes an incorrect or harmful decision.

The importance of addressing these ethical issues is therefore of vital importance. Ignoring or postponing them could not only lead to harmful consequences but also undermine public trust in AI, hampering its development and adoption.

Conversely, proactively addressing these issues can improve the effectiveness of technology, accelerate its responsible development, and maximize its positive impact on society.

It is a moral, legal and social imperative to consider ethics as a critical component in the evolution of AI, to forge a future in which technology serves as a force for good, rather than an amplifier of injustice and risk.

In conclusion, the urgent need to develop a robust ethical framework for AI is no longer an option, but an imperative. The ethical issues raised throughout this chapter are not abstract or speculative; they are immediately relevant and can have profound and long-term impacts on the well-being of society. And as AI continues to advance in leaps and bounds, the time to act is now. We cannot allow technological progress to exceed our ability to manage its ethical implications.

Creating an ethical framework for AI requires collective action, involving not only researchers, developers and policy makers, but also the public.

It is vital that these actors work together to define standards and guidelines that can provide a moral compass

for future development. It's not just about creating laws and regulations, it's about building a culture of ethics in AI that is intrinsic to the process of designing, developing and distributing the technology.

So this is a call to action. For developers, it's a call to responsibility to build systems that are not only intelligent but also ethical. For policy makers, it is a call to develop laws and regulations that are fair, transparent and accountable. For researchers, it is an invitation to continue exploring the frontiers of ethics in AI, thus providing help and direction for the most difficult questions. And for the public, it's a call to get actively involved in this dialogue, to ensure that the technology we're building is one that we want to live with.

AI has the potential to be one of the most transformative forces of our time, but only if we seriously and urgently address the ethical questions it raises. Let's take this moment not only as an opportunity to innovate, but also as a mandate to act with integrity and responsibility. The future of AI, and perhaps our society, depends on it.

To address these ethical issues, a multi-pronged approach is needed including rigorous ethical standards, government regulations, and stakeholder engagement. AI algorithm developers should work closely with physicians, patients, ethicists , and policy makers to ensure technologies are implemented ethically and responsibly. Independent third-party expert reviews could also be useful for assessing the fairness, accuracy, and safety of AI-powered medical algorithms.

# Chapter 6: Applications of AI in Industry

Artificial intelligence has now become an unstoppable force that is shaping the future of industry in ways few could have imagined just a decade ago. It's not just about automating processes or making operations more efficient; AI is rewriting the rules of how businesses work, creating new business models and altering entire industrial ecosystems. While early waves of technological innovation led to the standardization and automation of manual tasks, AI holds the promise of automating the decision itself, freeing up human creativity and innovation to focus on more complex and meaningful problems.

This transformation is as exciting as it is complex, as the implications of such pervasive use of artificial intelligence go far beyond mere operational efficiency. We are talking about a change that has the potential to affect key sectors of industry, from manufacturing and logistics to energy, from finance to health. Every industry is discovering unique and innovative ways to use AI to solve old and new problems. For example, AI can improve the energy efficiency of factories, personalize financial services for individuals and businesses, or even diagnose diseases at an early stage when they are most treatable.

However, it is important to recognize that this new AI-driven industrial landscape is infused with challenges and ethical issues that need rigorous attention. Large-scale automation could lead to job losses and create economic inequality. At the same time, the use of algorithms in decision making can introduce new types of bias or inaccuracy that can have serious consequences.

Last but not least, the growing interconnectedness and large-scale use of data raise questions about privacy and security which are of fundamental importance.

In this context, this chapter aims to explore the multiple facets of industrial applications of AI, not only highlighting the innovations and efficiencies it brings, but also probing the complex ethical issues that emerge from this new paradigm. The goal is to provide a comprehensive picture that helps navigate the rapidly changing industrial AI landscape, providing insights into both the opportunities and inherent challenges. Through this journey, we hope to come to a deeper understanding of not only what technology can do for us, but also what we should do with technology to ensure a sustainable and inclusive future.

It is imperative to examine how AI is transforming specific industries, giving birth to new paradigms that were unthinkable until recently.

## Applications in Manufacturing

Artificial Intelligence is playing a pivotal role in reinventing the modern manufacturing landscape, providing tools that go far beyond basic mechanical automation to enter the domain of decision, optimization and analysis. It's a breakthrough that's fueling what many experts have come to call Industry 4.0, a new era where manufacturing is not only automated, but also interconnected, adaptable, and intelligently optimized.

To appreciate the extent of this change, it is helpful to start at the beginning of the production chain. Traditionally, product design is a process that requires a significant amount of human time, resources and know-how. However, with the adoption of machine learning algorithms, manufacturing companies can now use AI to assist or even guide the design process.

For example, with the use of optimization and simulation algorithms, designers can get suggestions from the machine on how to improve the design to reduce material costs or increase product durability.

Once the product is designed, it moves on to the production phase, and here the AI is doing the same. Preventive maintenance is one area where AI has shown significant impact. Rather than following a regular maintenance schedule or reacting to machine failures when they occur, machine learning algorithms analyze data from sensors on machines to predict when a failure is likely to occur. This allows you to intervene earlier, reducing downtime and increasing operational efficiency.

Supply chain optimization is another key application. By using AI to analyze a wide range of variables, from market conditions to weather forecasts, companies can optimize their production and logistics plans to minimize costs while maintaining or improving service levels. In this way, AI can help create more resilient, flexible and adaptable supply chains.

But AI in manufacturing also goes beyond pure optimization and automation. We are starting to see the use of AI in mass customization, a paradigm where products can be tailored to specific customer needs without significantly increasing production costs. This is made possible by machine learning techniques that can intelligently coordinate and optimize manufacturing processes to handle a variety of customized products.

Of course, all of these innovations bring with them their own set of ethical and social challenges.

For example, advanced automation could lead to job losses in some areas of manufacturing, raising issues of social justice and inequality

economic. There is also a risk that AI could be used for worker surveillance in invasive ways, raising questions of privacy and dignity in the workplace.

Furthermore, as in all contexts where AI is used to make important decisions, there is a risk of errors, biases or even sabotage. This raises the need for robust governance, transparency and accountability mechanisms to ensure that the use of AI in manufacturing is ethical as well as effective.

So, as the manufacturing industry leverages AI to usher in a new era of efficiency, personalization, and innovation, it's critical to proactively address these and other ethical issues. Only through careful consideration of both sides of the coin – the technological potential and the ethical implications – can Industry 4.0 fully realize its promise to revolutionize manufacturing in a way that benefits all members of society.

Automation and industrial robotics have undergone a radical transformation thanks to the advent of artificial intelligence technologies. Once limited to simple, repetitive tasks, industrial robots can now handle more complex tasks that require some form of "intelligence". For example, AI-enabled computer vision systems allow robots to recognize objects and spatial orientations, making it possible to automate tasks such as selecting parts from a conveyor belt and placing them in a three-dimensional environment. This qualitative leap in functionality has led to an increase in operational efficiency in various industries. In the automotive sector, for example, robots now not only perform tasks such as welding and assembly, but can also perform quality inspections using computer vision to detect defects that could be overlooked by the human eye. This reduces the need for manual inspections, reducing both the time and cost of production.

Industries such as agriculture and logistics are also benefiting from advanced automation. Farming robots can now identify and remove weeds from a field, monitor soil conditions and even harvest fruit without damaging it, thanks to sophisticated handling systems. In the field of logistics, warehouse robots can autonomously navigate shelves, select items and prepare them for shipment – all much faster and more efficiently than traditional manual methods.

However, the growing adoption of automation and AI-powered robotics also raises ethical and social questions. The most immediate is the effect on the workforce. The automation of tasks previously performed by humans can lead to unemployment or underemployment, particularly for lower skilled workers. Furthermore, reliance on automated systems could lead to new types of risks, such as software malfunctions or vulnerabilities to hacking.

Another aspect to consider is the environmental impact. While automation can lead to more efficient processes that use fewer resources, manufacturing and maintaining robots and other automated systems requires materials and energy. Hence, it is essential to evaluate the long-term impact of these systems on our ecosystem. Industrial automation and robotics, powered by artificial intelligence technologies, are revolutionizing manufacturing and service delivery across a wide range of industries. However, it is crucial to address the complex ethical and social issues emerging from this revolution to ensure that benefits are distributed fairly and sustainably.

In the manufacturing industry, artificial intelligence is also revolutionizing the way goods are produced, processes managed and resources optimized.

Tesla is a notable example demonstrating how AI can play a crucial role not only in developing innovative products such as electric cars, but also in refining production methods. Tesla has implemented advanced algorithms to optimize the layout of its manufacturing plant and improve the supply chain. Use AI for preventive maintenance of machines, leveraging real-time data to predict any failures or maintenance needs. This allows the company to reduce downtime and increase overall efficiency, essential in such a competitive industry.

One could also consider the use of AI in robotic assembly lines, where computer vision and machine learning are used to improve product quality.

For example, high-resolution cameras coupled with deep learning algorithms can inspect products as they are being assembled, identifying defects with accuracy that surpasses human accuracy. This allows for more reliable production and improved product quality, while reducing costs associated with returns and repairs.

Process optimization and predictive maintenance, on the other hand, are two crucial applications of artificial intelligence in industry that aim to improve operational efficiency and reduce costs.

In process optimization, AI is used to analyze a large number of variables that could affect the output of an industrial process. Using machine learning algorithms, hidden patterns and relationships can be recognized between different variables, such as temperature, pressure, flow rate and other environmental factors.

Once these patterns are identified, the algorithm can suggest real-time adjustments to improve output quality or process speed.

For example, in a factory that produces plastic components, the AI could analyze data such as material temperature, machine speed and finished product quality to automatically adjust machine parameters and optimize production .

Predictive maintenance, on the other hand, focuses on predicting when a piece of equipment or machine will need maintenance or replacement, rather than waiting for a failure to occur. Traditionally, industrial maintenance followed a reactive or preventive model, where machines were either repaired after a breakdown or subjected to regular maintenance at set intervals. With predictive maintenance, sensors and AI algorithms continuously analyze the behavior and state of machines to predict potential points of failure before they happen. This allows companies to carry out targeted interventions, saving time and resources and minimizing downtime.

Both of these approaches use data gathered from a variety of sensors and other sources, which is then analyzed using machine learning techniques or advanced data analytics. The information obtained can be used not only to make immediate decisions but also to train further AI models, making systems even more intelligent and efficient over time.

Every example cited presents ethical issues that deserve careful attention. With advanced automation, such as that seen in Tesla, concerns arise about the future of work and whether machines will replace human workers. In the example of General Electric , the ethical aspect concerns who owns and controls the data generated by these critical infrastructures.

Ethical accountability is therefore not an afterthought, but a central element that needs to be carefully considered as AI continues to permeate
the manufacturing industry. Ethical implications need to be addressed proactively, through regulation, training and open dialogue between all stakeholders.

## AI in the Energy Sector

The use of artificial intelligence in the energy sector represents one of the most promising and transformative applications of the technology. While the energy sector has always been at the forefront of adopting new technologies, AI is starting to offer unique solutions that could hold the key to tackling some of the world's most pressing problems, such as climate change and energy security. The need for more efficient use of resources, together with the urgency to switch to more sustainable energy sources, makes AI a key tool for innovation in this field.

One of the most notable ways AI is contributing to the energy sector is through the optimization of energy generation and consumption.

For example, Google has partnered with DeepMind to use machine learning to reduce energy consumption in their data centers. By analyzing a large amount of data from sensors, the system is able to predict how variables such as temperature and pressure will affect energy efficiency and, consequently, automatically adjust cooling system settings to maximize efficiency. In doing so, Google said it reduced energy consumption for data center cooling by 40%.

Similarly, AI is being used to optimize efficiency in power plants. With sophisticated algorithms that analyze data in real time, it is possible to predict when a turbine needs maintenance or to adjust the angle of the wind generator blades to capture the wind more effectively. These optimizations may seem like minor details, but when implemented on a large scale, they lead to significant energy savings and reduced carbon emissions.

Energy demand management is another area where AI is showing remarkable capabilities. Machine learning algorithms can analyze historical and current consumption patterns to predict peak demand. These forecasts allow for a better allocation of resources and can also be used to inform consumers about the best ways to reduce their energy consumption. An example is the use of smart grids , smart electricity grids that use AI to optimally balance supply and demand. This dynamic balance can reduce costs for producers and consumers, while increasing the efficiency of the whole system.

Beyond these immediate applications, AI also has the potential to play a central role in the transition to renewable energy sources. With the urgent need to reduce greenhouse gas emissions, finding efficient ways to integrate renewable energy sources into existing energy systems is essential.

And here, machine learning algorithms can provide solutions for managing the intermittency of renewable sources such as solar and wind.

For example, an algorithm could predict energy production from a solar array based on factors such as weather forecasts and the angle of the sun, allowing a grid operator to decide how best to distribute energy among different sources.

Electric Corporation uses AI to improve the efficiency of its wind turbines.

Through the use of AI algorithms, GE is able to analyze a huge amount of data from sensors installed on the turbines to optimize performance and increase energy production.

This not only improves efficiency, but also reduces operating and maintenance costs, making wind energy a more competitive source of renewable energy. Also, there are companies like IBM that are using AI to predict and optimize energy generation and distribution. For example, the AI system can predict energy demand based on various factors, such as the weather, holidays and even sporting events. Based on these predictions, the system can then optimize power distribution to meet demand as efficiently as possible. A final example is the use of AI in the management of smart energy grids. AI can analyze real-time data from a variety of sources to better balance supply and demand, detect anomalies and prevent outages. Companies like Siemens are already implementing AI-powered solutions to make electricity grids smarter and more resilient.

These examples show how AI is not just a technological novelty in the energy sector, but a real driver of change, with the potential to radically transform the way we produce, distribute and consume energy.

However, the adoption of AI in the energy sector is not without its challenges. The issue of security is of primary importance, since the control systems of energy infrastructures are attractive targets for cyber attacks. Another crucial issue is the ethics of data collection and use, especially when it comes to sensitive data such as energy consumption of individual users.

A successful attack could not only compromise confidential information, but also disrupt the functioning of energy networks, with potentially catastrophic consequences.

It is therefore imperative that AI solutions in the energy sector are designed with robust security measures to protect against potential vulnerabilities.

Furthermore, there is the issue of transparency and accountability . While AI algorithms can optimize operations in ways beyond human capabilities, it is essential that experts understand how these decisions are made, especially when they have direct implications on energy access and costs for millions of people. This is especially true in contexts where AI is used to manage or allocate resources dynamically and in real time. Without an adequate level of transparency, it could be difficult for stakeholders, including regulators, to assess whether the algorithm is operating fairly or if it is, for example, discriminating against certain groups of consumers.

A further aspect to consider is the environmental impact of the AI itself. For example, the data centers that power these technologies consume large amounts of energy. While there is a broad focus on making these data centers as sustainable as possible, using renewable energy sources, it is a consideration that cannot be ignored in the larger context of energy sustainability.

Despite these challenges, the opportunities offered by AI in the energy sector are immense. In addition to the immediate efficiency and sustainability benefits, there is also the long-term potential to completely transform the way we think about energy production and consumption. AI can act as a catalyst for a faster transition to a more sustainable and resilient energy system.

In this regard, we are already seeing increasing investment in the research and development of energy-oriented AI solutions.

Universities, research institutes and companies are collaborating on projects ranging from optimizing power grids to using drones to inspect energy infrastructure such as power lines and wind towers.

We are likely to see an increasing number of startups focused on applying AI to the energy sector, thanks in part to the growing flow of capital from investors interested in supporting innovation in this vital field.

AI has the potential to revolutionize the energy sector in ways that were hardly imaginable just a few years ago. From optimizing existing infrastructure to facilitating the transition to more sustainable energy sources, the applications are vast and the implications profound. However, it is crucial to proactively address the security and ethical challenges associated with the use of AI, to ensure that this technological revolution translates into real and lasting benefits for all.

## Finance and AI

Artificial intelligence is revolutionizing the world of finance in ways that were unimaginable just a few decades ago. From the use of machine learning algorithms for algorithmic trading, to the use of big data analytics to assess credit risk, AI has become a key driver changing the face of the financial industry. Its application extends to numerous aspects, such as asset management , regulatory oversight, financial advice and even fraud detection. The potential for transformation is enormous, but as with any great revolution, there are also new ethical dilemmas and challenges that deserve careful consideration.

## Algorithmic Trading and Market Analysis

In the modern era of financial trading, AI algorithms have gone from simply automating manual tasks to making complex decisions in an extraordinarily short time.

This is partly due to their ability to perform operations in milliseconds, much faster than a human could. This speed becomes critical in environments such as high-frequency trading, where speed of execution can be the difference between a profit and a loss.

In addition to speed, the algorithms are designed to execute a variety of trading strategies which can be as complex as to include variables such as time spread, market volumes, prices and even real-time news. For example, there may be an algorithm that is programmed to buy a specific stock as soon as positive news is released from a credible source, all without any human intervention.

Another key aspect of algorithmic trading is the ability to customize and optimize algorithms based on specific trading styles or risk requirements. A pension fund that looks to the long term will have completely different needs from a hedge fund that operates on a day-to-day basis. In each scenario, algorithms can be fine-tuned to meet these needs, making possible strategies that would be too complex or too time consuming for humans to handle.

With the advent of big data, the potential for algorithms to access and use information has increased exponentially. Now they can analyze data from a variety of sources, including social media and weather data, to inform and refine their strategies. Analyzing sentiment from social media, for example, can provide valuable insights into market trends that haven't yet been priced into stock valuations.

Despite these benefits, algorithmic trading also comes with challenges. One of the main ones is the lack of transparency.

It's difficult for a human investor to understand exactly how an algorithm makes decisions, and this can lead to issues of trust and accountability. There is also the risk that algorithms could behave unexpectedly in extreme market conditions, with potentially significant implications for the stability of the financial system as a whole.

The growing role of algorithmic trading and market analysis implemented through AI involves not only technical but also ethical and regulatory considerations. One of the more pressing challenges is the potential for market abuse. Sophisticated algorithms can be designed to manipulate stock prices through strategies such as spoofing and quote box painting, which can mislead other market participants as to buying or selling intentions. Not only are these practices unethical, but they can also be illegal in many jurisdictions.

Another area that requires close scrutiny is the question of liability. In a market dominated by human trading, it is relatively easy to assign responsibility for trading decisions. However, in the context of algorithms, this attribution becomes less clear. If an algorithm causes a big loss or even a market crash, who is to blame? Is it the designer of the algorithm, the operator who ran it, or the machine itself? These are complex questions that require deep thinking and perhaps even new regulatory frameworks.

In the midst of these considerations, there is a growing recognition of the importance of transparency and interpretability of trading algorithms. Regulators are beginning to call for greater transparency in algorithmic operations. The goal is twofold: first, to ensure that companies fully understand the algorithms they are using; second, to allow for more effective monitoring of the market to prevent abusive behaviour.

Furthermore, the extensive use of algorithms and AI in algorithmic trading also raises issues related to cyber security. Because algorithms can execute transactions in fractions of a second, a cyber attack that manages to manipulate or even slightly hijack an algorithm can have catastrophic consequences. Therefore, the security of the algorithm and the data it uses becomes of paramount importance.

Let's not forget the constant technological advance that continues to push the boundaries of what is possible. With the introduction of deep learning techniques and other advanced forms of AI, trading algorithms will become more and more sophisticated. This offers new opportunities but also introduces new risks, including the possibility of unexpected errors or emerging algorithmic behavior that no human can anticipate.

Algorithmic trading and market analysis through AI represents a fundamental change in the financial landscape, offering enormous benefits in terms of efficiency and profitability. However, its growing pervasiveness introduces a series of complex issues ranging from transparency to accountability, from ethics to regulation. As a society, we are still in the process of navigating these uncharted waters, trying to balance the substantial benefits with the potential risks and ethical challenges that emerge in this new environment.

## Credit Risk and Management

Risk assessment and credit management are key aspects of the financial sector that are undergoing radical transformations thanks to the introduction of artificial intelligence technologies. The ability to collect, process and analyze massive amounts of data has allowed providers to financial services to revolutionize the way they assess customer creditworthiness, manage credit portfolios and prevent fraud.

To fully understand the impact of AI in these areas, it is helpful to look at traditional risk assessment techniques and how AI is improving them. Traditional credit scoring models often rely on a limited set of variables, such as income, employment, and past lending behavior, to make fairly broad predictions about the likelihood that an individual or company will be able to repay a loan.

However, these metrics can be incomplete and often ignore contextual or behavioral information that could provide a more accurate assessment of a customer's creditworthiness.

That's where artificial intelligence comes into play. Sophisticated algorithms, often based on machine learning techniques, can analyze a much wider range of data, including not just traditional financial information, but also purchasing behavior, social media interactions, and even geographic data. This allows for a much more holistic and personalized risk assessment, which can lead to more informed credit decisions and ultimately healthier credit portfolios for financial institutions. But as with all emerging technologies, the use of AI in risk assessment and credit management raises a number of ethical and regulatory issues. The first and most obvious is the issue of data privacy. Access to such a wide range of personal data for risk analysis can raise legitimate concerns about the use and custody of that information. Companies must therefore not only effectively protect this data, but also be transparent about how it is used.

In addition to privacy concerns, there is the problem of algorithmic discrimination. If risk assessment algorithms are trained on datasets that include implicit or explicit biases, these algorithms can perpetuate or even amplify these inequalities. For example, if an algorithm is trained on historical data showing higher default rates for certain ethnicities or geographic locations, it could unfairly penalize credit applicants from these groups or areas.

This is especially problematic because AI algorithms, once implemented, can operate at a scale and speed that can rapidly amplify the impacts of such biases . That's why it's crucial that companies and regulators pay attention not only to the accuracy of the algorithms, but also to their fairness and impartiality.

Another crucial aspect is transparency and accountability . With risk assessment models becoming increasingly complex, thanks to the integration of AI techniques, it also becomes more difficult for humans to understand how certain decisions were made. In the event of a dispute or error, this lack of transparency can become a significant problem. Financial institutions must therefore adopt tools and practices that not only improve the effectiveness of their algorithms, but also their interpretability and transparency.

AI is transforming risk assessment and credit management in ways that offer significant opportunities for greater efficiency and accuracy. However, these innovations also come with ethical and regulatory challenges that require careful consideration. The key to navigating this new landscape will be finding a balance between adopting new technologies and maintaining high ethical and regulatory standards. To what extent society and the industry are prepared to meet these challenges remains an open question, but one thing is certain: AI is here to stay, and its impact on the field of risk assessment and credit management will be deep and lasting.

The long-term implications of integrating AI in these areas are not only technological, but also social and cultural. As public trust in algorithms grows, so does the responsibility of financial institutions to ensure that these technologies are used ethically and fairly. One of the most pressing challenges is regulation. How can regulators keep pace with rapid and often exponential technological development? Existing credit and data privacy regulations are often insufficient to address the unique issues raised by AI. There is therefore a growing need for new regulatory frameworks that are flexible enough to adapt to technological changes, yet stringent enough to protect consumers' interests.

In recent years, the world of finance has been profoundly transformed by the adoption of artificial intelligence technologies.

For example, the use of machine learning in algorithmic trading has changed the way investors analyze and react to market data. Algorithms can now process massive amounts of data in real time, providing traders with an edge in speed and accuracy. Major companies such as Goldman Sachs and JPMorgan Chase have developed algorithmic trading platforms that use machine learning to adapt to market conditions in real time, improving the profitability of their trades.

These algorithms don't just execute buy and sell orders faster than humans; they can also analyze a wide range of variables that go far beyond stock prices. For example, they can take into account factors like market sentiment expressed on social media, economic news, and even weather conditions, to predict market movements.

This represents a paradigm shift from traditional methods of financial analysis, which tend to focus on a relatively small number of variables.

Another area that has seen significant impact from AI is risk management and compliance. For example, blockchain technology is often integrated with machine learning algorithms to improve transparency and reduce the risk of fraud. Major banks like Bank of America and HSBC have invested in AI technologies to improve their fraud prevention systems, using algorithms that can analyze user behavior patterns and identify suspicious activity with unprecedented accuracy.

Credit rating is another industry experiencing rapid evolution thanks to AI. Fintech companies like ZestFinance and Upstart use machine learning to analyze thousands of variables that go far beyond just your credit score.

This allows them to provide more personalized and potentially fairer loans, reducing risk for the lender and lowering costs for the borrower.

Some of these platforms also use non-traditional data, such as social media activity or online purchases, to assess an individual's creditworthiness, although this raises significant privacy and discrimination issues.

The growing adoption of AI in the financial sector is not without its challenges. There is heated debate about how to regulate these new technologies, with some voices calling for greater transparency in the algorithms used for financial decisions. Additionally, the growing reliance on automated systems raises concerns about vulnerability to new types of cyberattacks. However, it is undeniable that AI has the potential to make the financial sector more efficient, fairer and more resilient, provided these challenges can be adequately addressed.

The use of AI-powered chatbots has improved customer service efficiency, enabling banks to handle more inquiries with fewer staff. These chatbots can answer common questions, provide balance information, and help with transactions, freeing up human staff to tackle more complex issues. For example, Bank of America has launched a virtual assistant called Erica, which uses AI to help customers with a variety of banking transactions. Furthermore, AI is also revolutionizing the way financial institutions handle and analyze data. Machine learning algorithms can analyze massive amounts of data to spot patterns and trends that wouldn't be immediately apparent to a human analyst. This can help banks identify new market opportunities, improve their investment strategy and prevent possible risks.

An example of this is the use of AI in credit risk management. Algorithms can analyze a wealth of data, such as income, work history and spending behavior, to predict the likelihood that an individual will default on a loan. This allows banks to make more informed decisions about who should receive credit and at what interest rates.

Another application of AI in the financial sector is fraud prevention. Machine learning algorithms can analyze massive amounts of transactions in real time to identify suspicious behavior patterns that could indicate fraud. This allows banks to identify and stop fraudulent transactions before they cause significant damage.

However, despite its numerous benefits, the use of AI in the financial sector also raises some important concerns.

For example, there is concern that automation could lead to job losses, especially for lower-skilled workers. Furthermore, there is also concern that algorithms may incorporate unconscious biases , leading to unfair or discriminatory financial decisions. For this reason, it is important that algorithms are developed and tested carefully to ensure they are fair and transparent. Finally, there is also the question of security. As the use of technology increases, there is also an increased risk of cyber attacks. It is therefore imperative that financial institutions implement robust security measures to protect their customers' sensitive data.

AI has the potential to revolutionize the financial sector, making it more efficient, fairer and safer. However, it is important to address associated challenges, such as job losses, bias and security, to ensure the benefits of AI are fully realised.

The future challenge may also concern the issue of global equity. As AI becomes more advanced, there is a risk that only the largest and wealthiest financial institutions will be able to take full advantage of its benefits, potentially widening the gap between large players and small financial service providers. And what about developing countries? Will they be able to participate in this revolution, or will they be left behind, further exacerbating global inequalities?

In addition to regulation, there is an urgent need for education and literacy, both for industry professionals and the general public. Insiders need to understand the ethical implications of the decisions they are automating.

They must be able to interrogate an algorithm, understand its limitations, and intervene when necessary.

The public, in turn, must have a basic understanding of how these algorithms work and what their rights are in an increasingly automated world.

In any case, one thing is clear: while AI offers huge opportunities to improve risk assessment and credit management, it also brings with it a complex set of challenges that require concerted action from regulators, industry and civil society. To reap the full benefits of this breakthrough technology, we must proactively address these challenges, with a keen eye on the ethical principles that guide our interactions with technology and with each other.

# Chapter 7: AI in the Health Sector

Artificial intelligence is revolutionizing the medical industry in previously unthinkable ways, providing tools that empower clinicians and researchers alike. The ability to analyze huge datasets in short periods of time opens up new avenues for early diagnosis, personalized treatments, and even disease prevention. But as we embark on this new era, it is vital that we carefully examine the ethical, legal and social implications. The goal is to ensure that these technologies are implemented in a way that maximizes benefits while minimizing associated risks, such as those related to data privacy, equity in access to care, and accuracy of diagnosis and treatment.

## AI Assisted Diagnostics

Diagnostics is one of the most complex and crucial activities in medicine, often constituting the first step in determining an adequate treatment. Traditionally, diagnostics have been heavily dependent on the physician's expertise, clinical intuition, and ability to interpret a variety of clinical data. However, with the arrival of artificial intelligence in healthcare, the dynamic is changing rapidly. AI-assisted diagnostics represents a crossroads where technology and medicine meet to improve accuracy and efficiency, while offering new challenges and ethical questions for the medical community to address.

AI has been effectively used to interpret a variety of diagnostic data, including medical images such as X-rays, MRI scans and CT scans, DNA sequencing data, laboratory test results, and patient data from electronic health records.

In addition, specific algorithms can help doctors detect symptoms or abnormalities that may not be immediately apparent, allowing for more timely and accurate diagnoses.

Deep learning algorithms, a subcategory of machine learning, have shown particular promise in medical imaging. For example, deep learning algorithms have been trained to recognize signs of diseases such as breast cancer and age-related macular degeneration, often with an accuracy comparable or better than that of medical specialists. These algorithms can be particularly useful in resource-limited settings, where medical specialists may not be readily available.

However, AI-assisted diagnostics are not without challenges and concerns. One of these is the question of interpretation. While an algorithm can be highly accurate at recognizing a pattern on a scan, its ability to put this information into context may fall short of a trained clinician. For example, an algorithm might be able to identify a tumor, but it might lack the ability to consider other important factors, such as the patient's medical history or related symptoms, that could influence the final diagnosis and treatment plan.

Furthermore, there is the question of liability. In the event of a diagnostic error, it is crucial to determine whether the algorithm, the doctor who used the algorithm, or some combination of the two is to blame. This is a complex issue that has not only legal but also ethical implications, affecting trust in the healthcare system and the integrity of the medical profession.

There are also concerns about privacy and data security. Diagnostic algorithms require access to large volumes of sensitive medical data.

If this data were to fall into the wrong hands, there would be significant risks to patient privacy. Therefore, it is essential that strict protocols are in place for handling and protecting data.

Another ethical issue that emerges is that of equity in access to AI technologies. While advanced diagnostic systems may be available in well-funded medical centers, this may not be true for facilities in less developed areas. This creates a kind of 'diagnostic gap' which could worsen existing inequalities in health outcomes.

In the context of the continuous evolution of AI-assisted diagnostics, one of the most interesting areas is its application in complex and poorly understood diseases, such as neurodegenerative diseases or autoimmune pathologies. Often these conditions elude early diagnosis due to their insidious nature and non-specific symptoms. Here, AI has the potential to not only speed up diagnosis, but also to identify new markers or correlates that can be useful in finding new therapies.

The use of AI to make diagnostic predictions based on longitudinal data is also being explored. Imagine a system that can track an individual's health data over years and use this information to predict the likelihood of developing a certain condition in the future. This would open the door to a whole new dimension of preventive medicine.

However, these promises also bring with them new levels of ethical complexity. For example, if an algorithm can predict that an individual has a high probability of developing a serious disease, how should this information be handled?

And how can you ensure that they are not used in a discriminatory way by insurers or employers? The prospect of "data-based discrimination" is a real problem that needs to be addressed through stringent regulation. The "democratization" of diagnostics, where AI applications could be made available to the general public through smartphones or other devices, brings with it the risk of incorrect self-diagnosis and potential abuse.

While ease of access to diagnostics might seem like an advantage, without qualified medical advice, there is a risk that people could misinterpret the results, leading to increased anxiety or inappropriate treatments.

And we must not forget the importance of medical education. With the advent of AI-assisted diagnostics, medical education must adapt to equip future doctors with the skills to work in symbiosis with the technology. They should be trained not only on how to use these tools, but also on how to interpret their results and, above all, on how to maintain an ethical approach in using them.

In today's landscape, AI-assisted diagnostics is no longer a futuristic concept, but a tangible reality that is already influencing medical practice. Like any powerful tool, it comes with its own set of benefits and responsibilities. To maximize benefits and minimize risks, it is essential that the medical community adopt a thoughtful and multidisciplinary approach. We must proceed with caution, but also with some optimism, recognizing the transformative potential of AI to improve medical diagnosis and ultimately quality of life for patients around the world.

## Personalized Therapies and Precision Medicine

The concept of personalized therapies and precision medicine has always captured the imagination of physicians, researchers and the public. The idea that we could, one day, have a highly specific treatment for each individual, taking into account not only symptoms but also their genetic background, lifestyle and other variables, is revolutionary. With the rise of artificial intelligence, this future seems ever more within reach.

One of the major challenges of traditional medicine has been the "one size fits all" approach to medical treatments. Even with the most advanced use of diagnostics, physicians were limited by the quantity and quality of data they could collect and analyze. Artificial intelligence has changed this dynamic, allowing the analysis of huge datasets in incredibly short times. We can now, in theory, get a much more accurate picture of an individual's pathology, down to the molecular level, and thus target much more specific treatments.

The results of this approach have been impressive in several fields. Take, for example, the fight against cancer. AI algorithms are already helping to design more effective treatment plans by analyzing thousands of variables ranging from genes to cellular markers and even environmental data. This allows doctors to predict a patient's response to a particular therapy and make adjustments "on the fly", reducing side effects and increasing treatment effectiveness.

However, the use of AI in this context is not without ethical and practical challenges. One major obstacle is how to ensure that these personalized therapies are accessible to all, not just those who can afford to pay for advanced treatments.

The algorithm may be neutral, but if access to its benefits is limited by economic or social factors, then precision medicine risks becoming a luxury for the few, rather than a general improvement in medical care .

Another ethical consideration concerns data management. In order to perform at their best, precision medicine algorithms require a huge amount of sensitive data. The question of privacy and data security therefore becomes central. Who owns this data? How are they protected? And how can we ensure that they are not used for unethical purposes, such as discrimination based on genetic predisposition to certain diseases?

The issue of accountability is also crucial. If a personalized AI-based treatment were to fail or cause serious adverse effects, who should be blamed? Is it the doctor, who followed the recommendations of the algorithm, or is it the team of developers who created the algorithm itself? Or could it be the healthcare system that has adopted this technology without fully understanding its risks and limitations?

As AI-assisted precision medicine continues to evolve, the implications for medical education and the doctor-patient relationship become more and more relevant. With the advent of increasingly advanced diagnostic and therapeutic tools, how is it possible for doctors to keep up to date? It will be imperative that medical schools and continuing education programs adapt to prepare healthcare professionals to interact effectively with these new technologies. There could also be changes in the dynamics of the doctor-patient relationship, as artificial intelligence could take over some of the functions traditionally performed by the doctor, such as diagnosing and, in some cases, even prescribing treatments.

This also raises questions regarding patient autonomy.

The use of AI could theoretically improve patients' understanding of their health conditions by giving them access to more accurate and personalized information. However, there is also the risk that the complexity of the algorithms and data could make it more difficult for the patient to fully understand medical recommendations, potentially putting informed consent at risk.

And while AI has the potential to make medicine more precise and personalized, there is also a dark side: the possibility of overmedicalization. Algorithms could identify "anomalies" or "risks" that don't actually require medical intervention, leading to overtreatment or even harmfulness.

This is another reason why it is crucial to keep human doctors as an integral part of clinical decision-making: to provide that level of judgment and empathy that, at least for now, AI is unable to replicate. Finally, we must consider the long-term impact of the large-scale adoption of personalized therapies and precision medicine. While these technologies could revolutionize healthcare, they could also have destabilizing effects on the existing healthcare system. For example, the initial costs for developing and implementing such technologies could be very high, leading to questions about who should bear these costs and how they should be distributed within the company.

the introduction of AI in the field of personalized therapies and precision medicine is one of the most promising, but also the most complex, frontiers of modern healthcare. It presents incredible opportunities to improve quality of life and treatment efficacy, but it also comes with a number of ethical, legal and social challenges that we must address seriously and carefully. It is imperative that physicians, engineers, policy makers and the public collaborate to ensure these technologies are developed and implemented in a responsible, ethical and inclusive manner.

## Artificial Intelligence in Genomic Analysis

The advent of artificial intelligence has catalyzed a momentous transformation in genomic analysis, as the ability to decode and interpret massive amounts of data presents a challenge that goes beyond traditional computational and analytical capabilities. In addition to the extraordinary speed of analysis, AI introduces a previously unattainable level of precision and personalization. Genetics, once relegated to the realm of long-term laboratory research, is now a diagnostic and therapeutic driving force in clinical medicine.

The applications are diverse and cover a broad spectrum ranging from the early diagnosis of hereditary diseases and cancer to the design of targeted gene therapies.

The traditional approach to genetic analysis has been mostly manual and required a great deal of time to run, analyze and interpret the data. With the introduction of advanced machine learning algorithms, it is now possible to identify patterns and correlations that were previously obscure. This not only speeds up the analysis process, but also opens the door to new types of investigations. For example, convolutional neural networks , originally designed for image recognition, have been adapted to analyze DNA sequences, recognizing patterns and structures that can indicate the presence or absence of certain diseases or conditions.

The sophistication of AI algorithms has also made it possible to move beyond the analysis of single genes to explore the entire network of gene interactions.

This is crucial for understanding complex diseases such as cancer, cardiovascular disease and neurodegenerative diseases, in which multiple genes and environmental factors may play a role.

By analyzing these complex gene networks, AI algorithms can predict with unprecedented accuracy how variations in a single gene may affect the expression of other genes and, consequently, the overall disease profile .

Another area that is significantly benefiting from artificial intelligence is precision medicine. Treatments can be tailored to each individual's unique genetic profile, optimizing the likelihood of success and minimizing side effects. In the past, the approach was more generalized, based on symptoms and diagnoses that often did not take into account genetic differences between individuals. Now, AI can quickly analyze a genome and provide information that can help doctors choose the most effective treatment.

But while AI offers tremendous opportunities, it is vital to consider the ethical implications, especially in terms of privacy and informed consent. An individual's genome is the most personal information that exists, and its disclosure or misuse could have serious consequences. Therefore, issues related to genomic data custody, access and consent must be handled with utmost care. The balance between rapidly evolving innovation and ethical considerations will be a key part of the future of AI in genomic analysis.

This is just a taste of the reach and impact of AI in this industry. The conjunction of AI and genetics is breaking new ground that could fundamentally change the way we understand health and disease, offering opportunities that were once confined to the realms of science fiction. However, with great power also comes great responsibility, and the road to the full realization of this potential will be strewn with ethical, legal and social challenges which will need to be approached with care and consideration.

Artificial intelligence in genomic analysis is also paving the way for early identification and prevention of disease. In this context, predictive models can be built that signal genetic risk factors for specific conditions, such as susceptibility to breast cancer, cardiovascular disease or diabetes. Such models can also predict the likelihood that an individual will respond positively or negatively to a certain type of treatment. This could, in theory, save years of ineffective therapy and, in some cases, even lives. It's the kind of proactivity that was nearly unimaginable just a decade ago.

In regards to gene therapy, AI offers tools for designing more effective strategies for gene editing. This could be particularly useful in the treatment of hereditary diseases such as cystic fibrosis, muscular dystrophies and some forms of blindness.

Algorithms can simulate the effect of specific genetic modifications, allowing researchers to anticipate outcomes before therapies are even tested in the laboratory or in clinical trials. This represents a huge step forward in reducing the time and costs associated with the research and development of new treatments.

As we face these incredible possibilities, it is crucial to maintain an ethical focus. In addition to the data privacy concerns already mentioned, there is also the risk of genetic discrimination. If genomic data becomes public or is accessed by employers or insurers, it could be used in a discriminatory way. There is also the issue of 'genetic engineering', where the ability to modify genes raises ethical questions regarding the design of 'tailored babies', with ethical and moral implications that society as a whole must carefully consider.

The question of equitable access is also of vital importance. With the increasing commercialization of technologies related to AI and genomic analysis, there is a risk that only those who can afford such services have access to the benefits of personalized medicine. This could further exacerbate existing inequalities in the health care system, creating a gap between those who can afford advanced medical care and those who cannot.

The intersection of artificial intelligence and genetics offers a fertile field for innovation in diagnostics, therapy and prevention. But like every new frontier, it brings with it new risks and responsibilities. The challenge will be to navigate this complex landscape ethically and responsibly, ensuring that the benefits are spread as equally as possible. The implications of this technological revolution will be profound, and as a society, we must be prepared to manage the resulting changes, ensuring that science and ethics go hand in hand.

# Pharmacology and Drug Development

Pharmacology is the science that studies the interaction between chemical substances and biological systems, with a particular focus on the effect of these compounds on the functioning of the human body. Despite having ancient roots in traditional medicine and herbal medicine, pharmacology as a scientific discipline has made significant progress since the 19th and 20th centuries. In parallel with this evolution, drug development has become an increasingly complex and regulated process, requiring years of research and huge investments.

Before a drug can be developed, it is imperative to identify a molecular target in the body which could be an enzyme, a receptor or any other molecule involved in a metabolic pathway or disease process. This target must be studied in detail, using techniques such as X-ray crystallography, mass spectroscopy, and various other biochemical and biological methods to understand its structure and function.

Once the target has been identified, the next step is the discovery of candidate molecules that can interact effectively with it. Traditionally, this process was done through screening methods that evaluated one molecule at a time. Today, thanks to the advancement of technologies, it is possible to perform high- throughput screening, ie the simultaneous evaluation of thousands of molecules, to identify those with the greatest therapeutic potential. The selected molecules are then optimized through a series of chemical modifications to improve their efficacy, selectivity and safety profile.

Before proceeding to trials in humans, drug candidates must pass a series of preclinical studies. These include in vitro studies, often using laboratory-grown human cells, and in vivo studies in animal models. The aim is to evaluate the efficacy of the drug, its mechanism of action, and identify any toxic effects.

If a drug successfully passes the preclinical stage, the next step is human clinical trials. This phase is strictly regulated and requires the approval of ethics committees and health authorities.

Phase I: Phase I is primarily aimed at evaluating the safety of the drug and involves a small number of healthy volunteers. Pharmacokinetics, that is, how the drug is absorbed, distributed, metabolized and eliminated from the body, is studied.

Phase II: If Phase I proves the drug is safe, it progresses to Phase II, which involves a larger number of participants and focuses on how well the drug works for a given condition.

This phase also provides preliminary data on optimal dosage and side effects.

Phase III: In this phase, the drug is tested on even more patients, often at different research centers, to confirm efficacy, monitor for side effects, and compare the new drug against existing treatments or a placebo.

Phase IV: Even after approval, the drug continues to be monitored for long-term or rare effects that may not have been seen in earlier phases.

After passing all clinical stages, the drug can be submitted for approval to health authorities, such as the Food and Drug Administration (FDA) in the United States or the European Medicines Agency (EMA) in the European Union. These agencies painstakingly evaluate all data collected to determine whether the drug is both effective and safe. If it passes this test, the drug can be marketed and made available for prescription.

Even after approval, surveillance continues. This is known as pharmacovigilance. Physicians and patients are encouraged to report any adverse effects, and in some cases further post-marketing studies may be required. If new data on adverse effects emerge, the drug may be withdrawn from the market or its indications may be changed.

Drug development is a long, expensive and uncertain process. Even with advances in technology, most drug candidates never reach the market, often due to efficacy or safety concerns. However, new technologies such as genetic engineering, systematic biology and artificial intelligence are opening new frontiers in drug discovery and development.

One of the most immediate applications of AI is the " drug repurposing ", i.e. the search for new uses for existing drugs.

For example, machine learning algorithms have been used to identify existing drugs that could be effective against COVID-19. Many of these discoveries are still in the validation phase, but the approach has the advantage of being able to significantly speed up the development process.

In some cases, AI has been used to design new molecules with potential therapeutic applications. For example, startup Atomwise uses AI to predict which molecules might be effective at binding to certain biological targets. Atomwise 's platform has been used in various research projects to discover new drug compounds for a variety of diseases, from infections to cancers.

Several AI platforms, such as the one offered by BenevolentAI , focus on optimizing existing or in-development drugs. Using a wide range of data, from clinical studies to molecule databases, these platforms can predict how to make chemical modifications to a molecule to improve its efficacy, bioavailability or reduce its side effects.

AI is also used to tailor drug treatments to specific patient needs. Machine learning algorithms can analyze genetic data, biomarkers and other information to predict how an individual might respond to a given drug, allowing for more targeted and potentially more effective therapy.

AI has also facilitated new models of collaboration in pharmaceutical research. Projects such as OpenZika , which uses distributed computing power to search for new treatments for the Zika virus, integrate AI algorithms to analyze potential interactions between molecules and biological targets.

It should be noted that while AI offers enormous potential, the drug development process is complex and requires rigorous validation.

So while AI can accelerate discovery and development, proposed drugs still need to go through traditional clinical stages to prove their efficacy and safety.

The use of artificial intelligence (AI) in drug discovery and development has enormous potential for benefits, but as with many powerful technologies, there are also security and ethical risks associated with its misuse. One such risk is the possibility that AI could be used for malicious purposes such as creating new illicit drugs, poisons or chemical weapons. Some of these concerns are explored below.

AI has the ability to design molecules with specific chemical and biological properties. Theoretically, it could be used to design new narcotic or psychotropic substances that could circumvent existing legislation. For example, it may be possible to slightly modify the chemical structure of an existing illicit drug to create a new substance that is not technically illegal but has similar effects. This poses a huge legal and public safety risk, as these new substances may not have undergone rigorous testing to determine their safety or long-term effects.

In the military or terrorist context, AI could also be used to develop more effective poisons or chemical weapons. For example, it may be possible to use AI to identify compounds that are particularly toxic, stable and easy to produce, making it easier for malevolent actors to create chemical weapons.

The risk is not only related to the direct use of AI for nefarious purposes, but also to the security of the data and of the AI platforms themselves. A cyberattack that compromises a drug discovery platform could theoretically allow access to information that could be used in malicious ways.

Because of these risks, it is imperative that there are strict safety measures and ethical regulations around the use of AI in drug discovery. This could include restrictions on access to certain AI platforms, stringent security audits and the need for ethical reviews for research using AI to discover biologically active molecules.

Likewise, it is crucial for the international community to collaborate in defining ethical standards and guidelines for the responsible use of AI in sensitive contexts such as pharmaceutical research. This is especially important in an age where technology makes it increasingly easier for individuals or small groups to carry out activities that were once possible only for large organizations or nation-states.

While AI has enormous potential to do good, it is essential to be aware of the risks associated with its misuse. As with all powerful technologies, the key is responsible and thoughtful use, with proper consideration of the security and ethical implications.

Pharmacology and drug development are interdisciplinary and rapidly evolving fields that incorporate aspects of biology, chemistry, physics, and medicine. The ultimate goal is always to find safe and effective therapies that can improve the quality of life of patients.

## Monitoring Patients with Artificial Intelligence: A New Paradigm of Care

In an age where digitization has become an inescapable component of our daily lives, the field of medicine is no exception.

The advent of artificial intelligence (AI) is dramatically changing the way doctors and healthcare systems interact with patients.

One of the most promising aspects of this transformation is patient monitoring, which can now be augmented in ways that were once considered science fiction.

Traditionally, monitoring of patients has been done through periodic physical exams, blood tests, and other diagnostic tests. However, these methods only provide a "snapshot" of a patient's health status at any given time, which may not be sufficient to detect gradual changes or to predict critical events such as a heart attack or kidney failure episode. AI has the ability to analyze massive amounts of data in real time, opening up the possibility of continuous monitoring that can provide a more complete and dynamic picture of an individual's health.

One of the first applications of AI in patient monitoring was the integration with biometric sensors and wearable devices. For example, smartwatches and fitness bracelets can monitor various parameters such as heart rate, blood oxygen level and physical activity. This data, once collected, can be analyzed by AI algorithms to detect anomalies or worrying trends. But it goes further. We now have specialized medical equipment equipped with advanced sensors that can monitor everything from intracranial pressure to organ function in real time. These devices can be connected to AI systems that not only record data, but also interpret it in a clinical context.

What makes AI-based monitoring truly revolutionary is its ability to integrate and interpret data from different sources. For example, an algorithm could simultaneously analyze data from an EKG, levels of various biomarkers in the blood, and images from a CT scan to provide a diagnosis or early warning of a possible critical event, such as a heart attack.

Long-term data collection and integration is also of enormous value. Let's imagine a patient with diabetes and heart failure.

An AI system could continuously monitor both blood glucose levels and various heart metrics, adapting doses of insulin or other drugs in response to changes in heart rhythm or stress levels.

Personalization is another key aspect of AI-powered monitoring. Everyone has their own "normal" state of health, which can vary significantly from that of other people. AI algorithms can "learn" these individual normalities and adjust monitoring accordingly. For example, for a professional athlete, a resting heart rate of 40 beats per minute might be normal, while for an elderly, sedentary person, it could indicate a serious medical problem. AI can distinguish between these situations, reducing the risk of false alarms or missed alarms.

multi-parameter monitoring . For example, in a cancer patient undergoing chemotherapy, an AI system could monitor everything from hemodynamics to adverse drug reactions, adjusting the treatment regimen in real time to maximize both treatment efficacy and tolerability.

One of the traditional barriers to patient monitoring has been the difficulty of effective communication between physician and patient. In many cases, patients fail to accurately describe their symptoms or report changes in their health status in a timely manner.

Here, AI can act as a highly effective intermediary. Monitoring systems can send alerts to both patients and healthcare providers when anomalies are detected, facilitating timely and accurate reporting.

Furthermore, AI can also help 'translate' medical metrics into information that is more understandable for patients, improving their ability to actively participate in their own healthcare.

However, as with any powerful tool, AI-powered patient monitoring also presents ethical and practical challenges. One concern is data privacy.

With ever-increasing amounts of sensitive data being collected and analyzed, data security becomes a top priority. Algorithms must be designed with strong encryption and authentication features to prevent unauthorized access.

Another ethical issue is how to interpret and act on the data collected. For example, if an algorithm predicts a high risk of impending heart attack, what is the appropriate protocol for medical intervention? And what are the legal implications if the algorithm is wrong? These are problems that go beyond pure technology and require an interdisciplinary dialogue between doctors, ethicists , jurists and engineers.

In the broader context of public health, patient monitoring with AI has the potential to revolutionize not only individual care but also the management of healthcare resources. For example, during a pandemic, an AI system could monitor disease progression at the population level, helping health policymakers distribute resources such as ventilators or antiviral drugs where they are needed most.

However, it is crucial that access to these advanced technologies is equitable and does not contribute to existing health inequalities. Initiatives to implement AI-based monitoring therefore need to be accompanied by policies that ensure access for a diverse range of populations, including those that may not have easy access to advanced technologies.

Patient monitoring is one of the areas of medicine that is benefiting the most from the adoption of artificial intelligence. From the possibility of obtaining real-time data to the personalization of assistance; From expanding communication between doctors and patients to managing public health resources, AI offers a huge array of benefits that could transform our entire understanding of how healthcare is delivered. However, as with any innovation, it is crucial to proactively address the ethical and practical challenges that arise. Only through a balanced approach that integrates technology, ethics and public policy can we hope to realize the full potential of this extraordinary new tool.

# Telemedicine with Artificial Intelligence: An Ongoing Revolution

Telemedicine, a practice that allows remote medical advice via digital technologies, has assumed an increasingly central role in the global health landscape. In parallel, artificial intelligence (AI) has burst into numerous industries, transforming ways of doing things that have remained unchanged for decades or even centuries. When these two powerful tools meet, the result is a revolution in the way healthcare is delivered. In this chapter, we'll explore the implications of this synergy, touching on topics such as diagnosis, patient monitoring, ethics, and more.

One of the clearest applications of AI in telemedicine is in the field of diagnosis. Algorithms can analyze medical data, such as X-rays, electrocardiograms and genomic sequences, to provide fast and accurate diagnoses.

In some circumstances, the combination of telehealth and AI can even overcome the traditional limitations of the clinical setting.

For example, a dermatologist may have difficulty examining a rash through a video camera; however, a specialized AI algorithm could analyze a high-resolution image of the rash itself, providing a highly accurate diagnosis without the need for a physical exam.

This not only makes the diagnosis process more efficient but also opens up the possibility of providing specialized medical services in geographical areas lacking certain medical expertise. In a rural community without access to a neurology specialist, for example, an AI algorithm could analyze data from an EEG and provide a preliminary diagnosis of epilepsy, which can then be confirmed by a neurologist through a telehealth session.

We have previously discussed the role of AI in patient monitoring. This feature becomes even more powerful when combined with telehealth. Let's imagine a patient with chronic heart failure. Instead of going to the hospital for regular checkups, he may be wearing a device that continuously monitors various physiological parameters. This data would be analyzed in real time by an AI algorithm, which could send an alert to the treating doctor in case of anomalies. The doctor, in turn, could carry out a remote visit to evaluate the patient, thus avoiding onerous and stressful transfers for the latter.

Furthermore, AI has the ability to analyze large volumes of historical data, enabling a form of personalized healthcare that was unimaginable just a few years ago. For example, an algorithm could analyze years of blood sugar data from a diabetic patient and discover patterns related to diet, exercise, and other factors.

This information could then be used to optimize insulin doses or to suggest changes to the schedule lifestyle, all managed through periodic telehealth sessions with an endocrinologist.

A sticking point when it comes to telehealth and AI is the importance of the human aspect in healthcare. Despite the enormous potential of emerging technologies, medicine remains a science about people, with all their emotional and psychological complexities. Algorithms can diagnose diseases or monitor symptoms, but they cannot replace the doctor-patient relationship. For example, an algorithm might suggest that a patient with symptoms of depression should start drug treatment. However, only a physician can assess the larger context of a patient's life, including the potential underlying causes of depression and the patient's preferences regarding different treatment options. So while AI and telehealth can provide powerful tools for diagnosis and monitoring, they must be integrated into a system that values and respects each individual's uniqueness.

Like all technological innovations, the combined use of telemedicine and AI also carries risks and ethical concerns. One of the biggest hurdles is data security and privacy. Each telemedical interaction generates a large amount of sensitive medical data, which is then analyzed by algorithms. The security of this data is of the utmost importance, and any breach could have serious consequences not only for the individual patient but also for public trust in the entire healthcare system.

Furthermore, there is the question of liability in the event of diagnostic or treatment errors. In a traditional system, medical liability is relatively clear-cut. But in an environment where an algorithm could play a significant role in decision making, attributing accountability becomes tricky. These issues require scrutiny and the establishment of regulations and guidelines to ensure patients are protected.

Another ethical aspect to consider is the potential inequality in access to care. While telehealth has the power to bring specialized medical services to remote areas, there is also the risk that these technologies will only be accessible to those who can afford them, therefore creating an inequality in health care. It is therefore imperative that policies are in place to ensure equitable access to these services.

The conjunction of telehealth and AI also has a profound impact on the way doctors practice their profession. For example, the use of algorithms in diagnosing and monitoring patients could reduce physicians' workload, allowing them to focus on more complex cases and aspects of treatment that require human intervention. At the same time, the need to interpret and act on AI-generated data requires a new set of skills. Doctors of the future will need to be trained not only in medicine, but also in medical informatics, technology ethics and other related disciplines.

The intersection of telehealth and artificial intelligence represents one of the most significant changes in healthcare in recent years. This synergy offers enormous advantages in terms of efficiency, accessibility and personalization of the treatment. However, as with all emerging technologies, it also presents a number of ethical and practical challenges that need to be carefully addressed.

The key to making the most of the potential of this technological marriage is a balanced approach that takes into account both the possibilities offered by technology and the inherent complexities of healthcare. Only through an open, interdisciplinary dialogue between physicians, technologists, ethicists and public policy makers can we hope to successfully navigate these complex waters and harness the opportunities presented by telehealth and AI to improve healthcare for all.

The revolution is underway, and its implications are as vast as they are exciting. The path may be winding, but the rewards, in terms of lives improved and saved, are too great to ignore.

## Medical Records Management with Artificial Intelligence: A New Frontier in Digital Healthcare

Medical records have always played a vital role in healthcare, serving as a repository of a patient's medical information, past diagnoses, treatments, and responses to medications. Traditionally, this information was stored in paper format, requiring considerable physical storage space and making data sharing and analysis difficult. With the digitization of medicine, electronic health records (EHR, Electronic Health Records ) have radically changed the management of medical information. Now, with the advent of artificial intelligence (AI), we are entering a new era in medical record management. In this chapter, we will explore the emerging role of AI in medical record management, with a focus on aspects such as efficiency, personalization of treatment, and data security.

Simply digitizing medical records has not solved all the problems associated with their management. Indeed, it has often created new challenges, such as system integration and interoperability. This is where artificial intelligence comes into play. With AI, it is possible to process large volumes of data efficiently and derive useful insights from them. For example, algorithms can analyze medical records to identify patterns and trends, such as the response of certain patient groups to specific treatments. This analysis can then inform doctors about best practices and protocols to follow.

Furthermore, AI can facilitate the process of coding and categorizing information, an activity that can be very time-consuming for healthcare professionals. Advanced AI systems can automatically label and organize data such as lab results, clinical notes and imaging records , making the information easily accessible for healthcare professionals and for further analysis.

One of the most exciting promises of AI in medical record management is the ability to personalize medical treatments. Traditionally, medical decisions were based on general guidelines and the physician's experience. However, every patient is unique, with their own specific medical history, genetics, and responses to medications. Using machine learning algorithms, medical records can be analyzed to identify which treatments have been successful in patients with similar profiles. This information can then be used to develop a highly personalized treatment plan, thereby increasing the odds of a successful outcome.

AI can also play a role in continuously monitoring patients, using real-time data to update medical records and alert doctors to any signs of deterioration or adverse drug reactions. This way, decisions can be made quickly, sometimes anticipating problems before they become serious.

Medical record management comes with significant data protection and regulatory compliance responsibilities. Medical records contain highly sensitive information, and any security breach could have serious repercussions.

AI can help strengthen security through advanced encryption methods and monitoring of suspicious activity.

For example, an AI algorithm could monitor access to patient data in real time, reporting any

activity that seems out of the ordinary, such as logging in from unusual locations or browsing a large number of folders in a short amount of time.

However, the use of AI in medical record management also poses new ethical and legal challenges. Who is responsible if an algorithm makes a mistake that leads to inappropriate treatment? How can data privacy and security be ensured when it is shared with third-party algorithms for further analysis? These are questions that must be addressed with rigorous ethical and regulatory standards.

The use of artificial intelligence in medical record management is an exciting frontier with the potential to transform healthcare. It offers the promise of greater efficiency, more personalized treatments and better data security. However, it is also a field that presents new challenges and responsibilities. To realize the full potential of AI in this context, a holistic approach is needed that takes into account not only the technological capabilities but also the ethical and legal implications. Only through close collaboration between physicians, computer scientists, regulators and other stakeholders can we hope to successfully navigate this new era of digital healthcare.

Despite the many benefits that AI offers in medical record management, there are several technical and operational challenges that must be addressed.

One of the main challenges is the integration of existing systems. Many healthcare facilities already use medical record management systems, and integrating AI into these systems can be complex and costly. Some systems may not be compatible with new technologies, necessitating costly upgrades or even replacement of existing systems.

Furthermore, data quality is another critical factor for the success of AI in medical records management. AI algorithms are only as effective as the data they are trained on. If medical records are incomplete, inaccurate, or inconsistent, algorithms could generate erroneous or misleading results. Hence, it is essential to ensure that the data is of high quality and thoroughly curated before it is used to train algorithms.

Another operational challenge is the resistance to change by healthcare professionals. Adopting new technologies requires changing existing work habits and processes, which can be challenging for some people. Proper training and ongoing support are essential to ensure that healthcare professionals are comfortable with new technologies and can use them effectively.

To overcome these challenges and realize the full potential of AI in medical record management, close collaboration between different stakeholders is crucial. Algorithm developers, medical record management system providers, healthcare professionals, healthcare policy makers and patients themselves must work together to develop effective and secure solutions.

In particular, it is essential to involve healthcare professionals in the development and implementation process. They are the end users of the systems and therefore have a unique understanding of practical needs and operational challenges. Their experience and feedback can be invaluable in ensuring that the solutions developed are useful and functional in the real world of healthcare.

Furthermore, it is important to consider the impact on patients. AI has the potential to significantly improve patient care, but it is also essential to ensure that their data is treated with the utmost respect and protection. Transparency in data management must be ensured, and patients must have control over how their data is used.

Despite the existing challenges, AI has huge potential to revolutionize medical record management and ultimately healthcare in general. With the right collaboration, training and implementation, AI can help make healthcare more efficient , effective and personalized.

However, it's important to remember that AI is not a cure-all. While it may offer powerful tools for data analysis and clinical decision-making, the judgment and experience of healthcare professionals will always remain critical. AI should be seen as a complement to human capabilities, rather than a substitute.

Ultimately, AI in medical record management represents an exciting frontier that can bring significant benefits to both healthcare professionals and patients. With the right approach, we can overcome existing challenges and build a future where AI helps improve the quality and effectiveness of healthcare for all.

## Mental Health and Artificial Intelligence: A Synergy for the Future of Psychological Well-Being

Mental health is one of the most pressing issues of our time, with growing numbers of people around the world suffering from ailments such as depression, anxiety and stress. Traditional treatment modalities, which include psychological and pharmacological therapy, can be effective but also expensive, inaccessible and stigmatised. Artificial Intelligence (AI) is emerging as a new tool that has the potential to revolutionize how we address these challenges.

From applications that provide instant emotional support to advanced systems that assist professionals in diagnosing and treating, AI is breaking new ground in mental health.

Diagnosis is often the first step in treating any mental health disorder. Traditionally, this process has been based on detailed interviews and standardized tests administered by mental health professionals. However, thanks to AI, we are seeing the development of screening tools that can identify signs of mental health problems faster and, in some cases, more accurately. For example, machine learning algorithms can analyze data from a variety of sources, such as text, voice and even facial expressions, to identify behavioral or expressive patterns associated with particular mental disorders. This not only makes the screening process more efficient but can also help reach people who may not have access to qualified mental health services.

One of the most direct applications of AI in mental health is the provision of emotional support through chatbots and mobile applications. While these platforms cannot replace comprehensive therapy with a trained professional, they do offer a first level of care that can be invaluable. These platforms use natural language processing and other algorithms to provide instant, personalized responses to users who may need assistance in times of crisis. This type of immediate support is particularly helpful for those living in remote areas or for those who are reluctant to seek help due to the stigma associated with mental health issues.

Despite the growing availability of AI-based tools for mental health, the role of mental health professionals remains central. However, AI can serve as a powerful complement to human expertise. For example, advanced algorithms can analyze clinical notes, test data and other information to provide a more complete picture of a patient's psychological well-being.

This can help therapists tailor treatments and even predict how a patient might respond to particular treatment approaches.

Similarly, AI can assist in managing the workload of mental health professionals, often overwhelmed by large patient numbers and the bureaucracy associated with clinical management. By automating some of the more routine tasks, such as recording and analyzing patient data, AI allows therapists to focus more on the human aspect of care.

While AI offers significant opportunities in the mental health field, it also presents a number of ethical and technical challenges. One major point of concern is data privacy. Mental health information is extremely sensitive and its unauthorized disclosure could have serious consequences for the individual concerned. While AI can improve data security through advanced encryption and authorization techniques, the risk of privacy breaches remains a valid concern.

Another ethical issue is that of responsibility. If an algorithm suggests a treatment plan that turns out to be ineffective or harmful, who is to blame? These dilemmas require deep reflection on how AI is implemented and governed in the context of mental health.

Artificial intelligence has the potential to radically transform the field of mental health, offering new tools for diagnosing, treating and managing mental disorders. However, enthusiasm for these new possibilities must be balanced with careful consideration of the ethical and technical implications.

The future of mental health with AI is promising but also loaded with responsibility.

As technology advances, it is essential that physicians, engineers, policy makers and patients work together to navigate the complex landscape of opportunities and challenges.

The combination of medical, technological and human expertise is essential to ensure that AI-powered innovations are developed and implemented ethically and sustainably.

One of the most exciting areas for future research and development is the intersection between AI and personalized therapies. At present, most mental health treatments are generalized, based on standard protocols that do not account for individual variations. AI has the potential to change that, using massive data and advanced algorithms to create personalized treatment plans that are more effective and reduce the chance of negative side effects.

The issue of accessibility is also of vital importance. AI-powered tools could reduce costs associated with mental health care, making it more accessible to a wider audience. This is particularly relevant for communities in rural areas or for people in developing countries where access to skilled services may be limited.

However, we must not forget that AI is a tool, not a panacea. While it may offer new ways of care and diagnosis, it cannot and should not replace the importance of the human touch in mental health care. The therapeutic relationship, built on trust and empathy, remains a central element in the treatment of mental disorders. In this context, AI must be seen as a complement that can enhance, but not replace, human intervention. Furthermore, as we move forward in the incorporation of AI into clinical practice, it is imperative that there are rigorous standards for evaluating the effectiveness of these technologies. Well-designed clinical studies, peer reviews, and post-implementation monitoring are all necessary steps to ensure that AI-based tools are not only innovative, but also safe and effective.

AI offers an unprecedented opportunity to improve the quality and effectiveness of mental health treatment. Its applications, from automated diagnoses to digital emotional support, could revolutionize the way we address some of the most pressing issues of our time.

But to fully realize this potential, it is essential that we address the many complex challenges this new frontier presents, from ethical issues such as privacy and liability, to technical issues such as data integration and security. With a thoughtful and multidisciplinary approach, we can use AI to significantly improve mental well-being globally.

Resource Planning with AI in the Healthcare Environment

Healthcare resource management is one of the most complex and critical challenges facing modern organizations. From the scheduling of medical and nursing staff shifts, to the management of medical supplies, up to the maintenance of diagnostic and treatment machinery, every aspect requires careful and detailed planning. The arrival of artificial intelligence (AI) has opened up new horizons of possibilities, promising to revolutionize the way healthcare resources are allocated and managed.

One of the major benefits of employing AI in this context is its ability to analyze massive amounts of data to extract actionable insights. For example, in large hospitals, where patient flows can vary widely, AI can accurately predict the busiest times. This type of information is invaluable when it comes to scheduling staff shifts or deciding when to perform maintenance on critical machinery, such as intensive care beds or medical imaging equipment .

Similarly, AI can play a crucial role in managing medical supplies. By analyzing historical data on past uses and integrating information on epidemiological trends, AI can help prevent shortages or overabundances of critical supplies such as medicines, personal protective equipment and specialized equipment.

Another area where AI shows great potential is personnel management. Through sophisticated algorithms, staff skills can be matched to clinical needs, ensuring that people with the right qualifications are assigned to the most suitable tasks. This not only improves efficiency, but can have a direct impact on the quality of care provided.

For example, in a congested emergency department, an AI-based system could identify in real time which doctors and nurses are available and which ones have the specific skills to treat the most urgent cases. This allows for a deployment of human resources that is both dynamic and highly specialized, two factors often crucial in emergency situations.

Despite the enormous potential, the use of AI in healthcare resource planning also presents several challenges. One of these is the ethical aspect, particularly in terms of decisions that could directly affect the well-being of patients. For example, if an algorithm suggests reducing staff during certain hours based on historical data, there is always the risk that an unexpected event could lead to an influx of patients and, therefore, a shortage of human resources.

Another consideration is that of data security and privacy. As AI requires access to large volumes of sensitive data, it is imperative that stringent measures are implemented to protect this information from potential breaches.

The introduction of artificial intelligence into healthcare resource planning is an ongoing revolution that offers immense potential to improve the efficiency and effectiveness of care. Machine learning algorithms and data analytics techniques can provide valuable insights that go far beyond human capabilities, especially when it comes to processing large volumes of information. However, it is vital to proceed with caution, bearing in mind the ethical and practical challenges this new technology presents.

With proper planning and governance, AI has the potential to fundamentally transform healthcare resource management, leading to a more agile, more responsive, and ultimately more patient-centric system. While initial implementations of AI in healthcare resource planning may show promise, it's critical to maintain a constant feedback loop to refine and improve the algorithms over time.

This is especially true in healthcare, where variables can change rapidly due to factors such as epidemics, updates in treatment guidelines, or new drugs and technologies. A system that is not properly monitored or updated can quickly become outdated, leading to inefficiencies or, in the worst case scenario, risks to patient health.

Here's where AI itself can play a role in self-improvement. Machine learning techniques can be applied to analyze the performance of the algorithm itself, identifying areas where it could be improved. For example, if an algorithm designed to predict the influx of patients in an emergency room proves inaccurate during a particular time of year, the data could be used to train the model further, making it more accurate in the future.

Another crucial aspect to consider is the relationship between AI and human judgment. Despite the advanced sophistication of algorithms, context and human understanding remain irreplaceable, especially in a field as sensitive as healthcare. Healthcare professionals can provide that level of insight and empathy that a machine, however advanced, cannot replicate. Thus, the optimal view for implementing AI in healthcare resource planning is one of complementarity rather than substitution. Algorithms can process data and make recommendations, but the final decision should always be made by skilled humans, taking into consideration not only quantitative data but also qualitative variables that a machine might not be able to understand.

As we discuss AI in resource planning, it's also important to note that its potential in healthcare is much broader. In addition to improving operational efficiency, AI is also starting to be used in direct diagnosis and treatment, from analyzing medical images to identifying possible treatment plans based on analyzing patient data. This natural evolution of AI in the industry offers a vision of the future where AI could become an integral part of patient care, going far beyond just the role of resource planner.

The integration of artificial intelligence in resource planning in healthcare is an opportunity that offers both in terms of improving efficiency and quality of care. However, as with any powerful tool, it comes with its own set of challenges that need to be carefully managed.

Continuous monitoring, updating, and robust data governance are essential to ensure algorithms remain accurate and useful over time.

At the same time, it is crucial that AI is seen as a complement to human judgment, rather than a replacement for it. With these precautions, AI has the potential to become a pillar in the future evolution of the healthcare system, making it not only more efficient but also more centered on patient well-being.

## Medical Research with Artificial Intelligence: The Frontier of the Future

The era of artificial intelligence (AI) has brought with it a revolution in several sectors, and medical research is one of the fields that has seen the most significant transformations. The intersection of artificial intelligence and the medical field has ushered in new avenues of scientific inquiry, accelerating discoveries that, with traditional methods, could have taken decades to make. From analyzing complex data for drug discovery to predicting the progression of chronic diseases, AI is changing the way we address the greatest medical challenges of our time.

One of the most exciting aspects of applying AI to medical research is in drug discovery. Traditionally, this has been an extremely time-consuming and expensive process, often requiring years of experimentation and a large amount of investment. AI, with its ability to analyze and interpret large datasets, can significantly speed up this process.

Sophisticated algorithms can examine molecular interactions, predicting how certain combinations may react in the human body. Not only does this speed up the initial screening phase for potential new drugs, but it can also lead to more targeted discoveries, reducing the number of errors and failures.

Another area where AI is making significant progress is diagnostics. Machine learning tools

they can analyze medical images with an accuracy often superior to that of humans, identifying signs of diseases such as cancer, heart disease and neurological disorders in very early stages. This not only allows for early intervention, but also opens the door to more personalized therapies. If an algorithm can accurately identify the shape and stage of a tumor, for example, it is easier for doctors to choose the most effective treatment for that particular case.

In addition to diagnostics, AI can play a role in analyzing clinical data to personalize treatment plans. By analyzing patient information, such as genetics, medical history, and response to previous treatments, the algorithms can suggest treatment options that are more likely to be successful for that individual.

AI also has enormous potential in the field of epidemiology, the study of the distribution and determinants of disease within populations. Advanced algorithms can analyze data from a variety of sources, such as medical records, social media and environmental sensors, to predict the spread of infectious diseases. This type of modeling can be invaluable for epidemic or pandemic preparedness and response, enabling health policymakers to more effectively allocate resources and implement control measures before the disease spreads further.

Despite its promise and progress, the use of AI in medical research is not without its ethical challenges and dilemmas. Data privacy is a major concern, especially when algorithms need access to detailed medical data.

Cybersecurity therefore becomes a crucial consideration in protecting sensitive patient information.

While AI can be extremely accurate, it's not infallible.

Diagnostic or prediction errors can be serious consequences when it comes to human health.

It is therefore crucial that AI-generated results are interpreted and applied carefully, often in combination with human expertise.

The integration of artificial intelligence into medical research represents one of the most exciting frontiers of modern science. The potential applications are vast and could lead to significant improvements in disease prevention, diagnosis and treatment. However, as with any new technology, it is vital to proceed with caution, taking into consideration the ethical and practical challenges that arise.

Collaboration between AI experts and medical professionals will be the key to fully exploiting the potential offered by this revolutionary technology, carefully navigating between opportunities and risks. With the right focus and rigor, AI could very well be the key to unlocking new levels of understanding and treating disease, leading medicine into a new era of efficacy and personalization.

In addition to the more traditional domains of medical research, AI is also starting to shed light on emerging fields such as regenerative medicine. This field focuses on developing methods to regenerate damaged tissue and organs, with the ultimate goal of curing conditions that are currently intractable. The complexity of this area, which requires a deep understanding of cellular interactions, tissue biology and biomedical engineering, makes AI a particularly valuable tool. Machine learning and neural networks can, for example, help model how stem cells differentiate into different tissue types, accelerating the time it takes to bring new therapies from the laboratory stage to clinical practice.

Genetic analysis is another field where AI is demonstrating a game-changing capability.

Decoding the human genome has been a monumental work that has required years of collaborative effort. Now, thanks to AI, analyzing the vast amount of genetic data has become faster and more accurate. This has direct implications not only for understanding inherited diseases but also for interpreting how genes influence response to treatments. In an era where personalized medicine is increasingly becoming a reality, the ability to rapidly analyze genetic data to tailor treatments could have a far-reaching impact on the quality of healthcare.

One of the beauties of AI is its ability to facilitate interdisciplinary collaboration. Medical research projects that once would have required the expertise of specialists in various fields can now benefit from the analytical power of AI. For example, algorithms can review clinical data, radiology images, lab results, and physician notes, providing a holistic view of the patient. This is especially useful in multi-center clinical trials, where data comes from multiple sources. AI algorithms can smooth this data consistently, allowing for more robust analyzes and more reliable results.

As AI continues to shape the future of medical research, the challenges ahead are becoming ever more complex. One of these is the ethics of using AI in clinical decision making. To what extent should we allow machines to make decisions that directly affect human health and well-being? And how do we ensure that AI is used fairly, without amplifying existing inequalities in healthcare?

At the same time, the issue of transparency and accountability is increasingly urgent. As machine learning algorithms become more complex, it also becomes more difficult to understand how they are actually making their decisions, a phenomenon known as a "black box".

This opacity may not be acceptable in a medical setting, where decisions can have life-and-death consequences.

There is no doubt that artificial intelligence will have a lasting impact on medical research.

Its applications are vast and growing, offering an array of tools that can accelerate discovery, improve accuracy, and increase efficiency. But as with any powerful tool, it also comes with a responsibility to use it wisely. The ethical and practical challenges emerging from the convergence of AI and medical research require an open and ongoing dialogue between physicians, researchers, ethicists and policy makers. With the right amount of prudence and collaborative effort, AI can act as a catalyst in our eternal journey to understanding and improving human health.

# Chapter 8: AI in the Transport and Mobility Industry

Mobility is one of the foundations on which modern society rests, an essential gear that moves people, goods and information through an increasingly complex and interconnected network. Over the past decades, the transportation industry has seen significant advances, from the introduction of safer and more efficient aircraft to the evolution of public and private transportation. However, while traditional technologies have reached a certain degree of maturity, a new player is emerging with the potential to revolutionize the way we think about mobility: artificial intelligence.

AI is no longer a mere object of fascination in science fiction or an abstract concept debated in academic circles. It's a real, tangible change that's impacting multiple industries, from financial services to healthcare. But it is in the transport and mobility sector that artificial intelligence has shown some of its most promising and revolutionary applications.

Consider, for example, navigation systems. Once upon a time, having a paper map in your dashboard was the pinnacle of sophistication in terms of driver assistance. Today, thanks to artificial intelligence, our devices not only show us the best route to reach a destination, but also predict traffic, suggest alternative routes in real time and can even warn of traffic accidents before we pass them. These advances are made possible by the ability of AI to analyze massive amounts of data from different sources, such as sensors, cameras and historical data, to generate accurate and timely information.

But AI doesn't stop at making our lives easier on our daily commute. The way goods are transported is also changing, revolutionizing logistics and the supply chain. Machine learning algorithms can now accurately predict when a vehicle needs maintenance, reducing downtime and increasing operational efficiency. In the maritime navigation sector, intelligent systems are used to optimize ship routes, taking into account variables such as weather conditions and ocean currents, all to ensure faster and cheaper delivery of goods. However, perhaps the most fascinating and controversial aspect of the intersection of AI and mobility is the development of autonomous vehicles. These vehicles, often touted as the pinnacle of transportation innovation, are fundamentally based on highly advanced artificial intelligence systems that can 'see', 'think' and 'react' like a human - if not better. Through the use of sensors, radar and lidar, coupled with deep learning algorithms, these machines are beginning to navigate complex environments, holding the promise of safer roads and more efficient transportation.

This development of autonomous vehicles is not just about cars. It is also impacting other means of transportation such as trucks, trains and even ships. In aviation, for example, AI is already being used in pilot assistance systems and is starting to show its potential in more advanced applications, such as delivery drones and even unmanned aircraft.

Of course, the adoption of AI in the transportation sector also raises a number of important questions, including safety, ethics and employment. Despite these concerns, there is no doubt that artificial intelligence has ignited a new era in the history of transportation and mobility.

AI is set to shape the future of how we get around, how we interact with our environment, and how we build a more efficient and sustainable society. Its role is not just to be a technological facilitator, but a catalyst for deeper changes that will impact economic, social and even cultural aspects of our world. And so, as we continue to navigate this new era, it is crucial that we understand and appreciate the growing importance of artificial intelligence in shaping the future of transportation and mobility. On the one hand, it is a factor of great excitement, but it is also a call for caution and reflection on how to steer this powerful tool towards a future that is not only technologically advanced, but also socially and ethically responsible.

Artificial intelligence is moving beyond the scope of individual applications to become a sort of support infrastructure for the entire transport and mobility system. In the context of smart cities, for example, AI is becoming an indispensable tool for urban planning and service management. Machine learning algorithms can analyze complex patterns in the movement of people and vehicles, providing valuable data that can be used to improve everything from traffic light times to bus routes. This form of integrated management can significantly reduce traffic congestion, improve air quality and increase the overall efficiency of the transportation system.

But it's not just the public sector that benefits from artificial intelligence. Even private companies are starting to recognize the value of AI as a tool to improve operational efficiency and customer satisfaction experience .

For example, airlines are using AI to optimize flight itineraries, thus reducing delays and expenses.

At the same time, personalized recommendation algorithms can improve the traveler experience by suggesting travel options, accommodations, and even recreation based on personal preferences and historical data.

As AI continues to evolve, so does the need for standards, regulations and ethical guidelines to govern its use. The growing reliance on AI-powered systems makes it imperative to address issues such as data security, privacy, and the possibility of algorithmic errors or biases. And then there is the increasingly pressing question of the impact of automation on employment. While autonomous vehicles and intelligent traffic management systems can improve efficiency, there is also concern that these advances could lead to job losses in industries such as truck driving, taxi services and even management. of air traffic. However, it is essential to note that every new technology brings with it both challenges and opportunities. AI is no different in this regard. The key is finding a balance, where technology can be used to improve safety, efficiency and quality of life, without sacrificing core values such as equity, employment and human dignity. This is the task ahead of us as we move further into the age of artificial intelligence applied to transportation and mobility.

AI is radically transforming the transportation and mobility industry in ways we could only have imagined a few decades ago.

From autonomous driving and traffic optimization to supply automation chain and personalization of user experience, the applications of AI are vast and constantly evolving.

As we face the inevitable ethical and social challenges that emerge from this transformation, it is vital that we continue to explore the potential that AI offers, not just as a technological tool, but as a catalyst for meaningful and sustainable change in the way we live. we work and we move. And, as we do so, it's imperative that we keep in mind the immense responsibility of using this powerful technology in a way that benefits society as a whole, now and for generations to come.

# Automation and Autonomous Vehicles

Automation and autonomous vehicles are perhaps one of the most remarkable and talked about advances in the transport and mobility sector, and this is largely thanks to artificial intelligence. AI is fueling a quiet but persistent revolution, one that has the potential to rewrite the rules of mobility and redefine our relationship with road transport. This transformation is not a futuristic event that will take place in the distant future, but a tangible reality that is already unfolding before our eyes.

We begin with a look at the technological advancement behind autonomous vehicles. Just a decade ago, the idea of driverless cars navigating the streets autonomously was the subject of science fiction stories. Today, thanks to rapid advances in sensor technology, image recognition, and deep learning algorithms, these cars are now an experimental reality. High-resolution cameras, radars and lidars (light-based remote sensing technology) act as the vehicle's 'eyes' and 'ears', while machine learning algorithms process this data in real time to make route decisions , speed and other maneuvers. But what impact are autonomous vehicles having on businesses and consumers?

Take for example Uber and Tesla, two protagonists in this rapidly evolving space. Uber , originally a ride- sharing service , has invested significantly in autonomous vehicle technology with the goal of reducing operating costs and increasing safety. While promising results have been achieved in trials, the road to large-scale adoption is still long and littered with regulatory and societal hurdles. However, the promise is clear: a future where passengers can require a driverless car to get around efficiently and safely represents a paradigm shift.

Tesla, on the other hand, has taken a slightly different approach. Instead of focusing solely on fully autonomous vehicles, the company has developed a suite of driver assistance features, known as " Autopilot ," that can handle some driving functions but still require human oversight. While this does not represent complete autonomy, it is still a significant step towards it and serves as an effective entry point for consumers who are still hesitant about giving up control of the vehicle entirely.

In addition to Uber and Tesla, numerous other pilot programs are emerging around the world. In some cities, small autonomous vehicles are already delivering food and parcels, while in some industrial areas, autonomous trucks are employed to transport goods over long distances. These use cases show that vehicular automation is not limited to passenger vehicles but extends across the entire range of mobility, from last- mile delivery to heavy haulage.

Of course, the road to large-scale adoption of autonomous vehicles is far from smooth.

In addition to technological hurdles, such as the need for more precise algorithms and more reliable sensors, there are also a number of societal and regulatory concerns to address. The issue of safety obviously comes first.

Accidents involving autonomous or semi-autonomous vehicles fuel the debate about when and how these vehicles should be regulated. There is also the issue of employment impact, as vehicular automation could reduce the need for professional drivers.

Automation and autonomous vehicles are bringing about a revolution in the world of transport and mobility, a revolution driven in large part by artificial intelligence.

With companies like Uber and Tesla at the forefront and a myriad of emerging applications, we're starting to see the contours of a future where mobility is safer, more efficient, and perhaps even more affordable.

However, as we hurry into this exciting future, we must also address the challenges and concerns that emerge, so that the transition is not only technologically smooth, but also socially and ethically responsible.

The potential of a future where mobility is sustainable, efficient and accessible is a vision shared by many people. However, as with any technological revolution, automation and autonomous vehicles bring with them their own set of ethical questions that demand thoughtful answers. For example, how is liability determined in the event of an accident? In an emergency situation, how should an autonomous vehicle behave? These questions require deep ethical and legal reflection, and solutions must be found before technology becomes ubiquitous.

Another critical aspect is the question of equity in mobility. While automation has the potential to make transportation more efficient and cheaper, there's also the risk that some communities could be left behind.

For example, autonomous vehicles may initially be deployed in affluent urban areas, while rural communities and economically deprived neighborhoods may have to wait much longer to see the benefits of this technology.

It is therefore essential that policy makers and industry stakeholders work together to ensure inclusive adoption.

AI is also having a major impact in public transport. Metros and trains are starting to use AI to optimize schedules and improve passenger flow, while driverless buses are already being tested in some cities. The goal is to create a more integrated and responsive public transport system, where AI can help mitigate problems such as overcrowding and delays.

In aviation, AI is finding applications in everything from aircraft preventative maintenance to air traffic management. AI systems can analyze massive amounts of data to predict when specific parts of an aircraft might fail, enabling proactive maintenance that can improve both safety and efficiency.

Furthermore, AI can assist air traffic controllers in managing more efficient routes, thereby reducing delays and minimizing the environmental impact of flight.

Shipping is also starting to explore the possibilities offered by artificial intelligence. With the adoption of AI-assisted navigation systems, risks such as collisions and groundings can be significantly reduced. Furthermore, AI can be used to optimize the fuel consumption of large vessels, offering not only economic savings but also reducing the environmental impact of the industry.

The intersection of artificial intelligence, automation and transportation is one of the most promising and complex areas of the modern technological revolution. From cars to subways, planes to ferries, AI has the potential to make our transportation systems safer, more efficient, and more sustainable.

But as with any great technological leap, there are also significant challenges ahead, both technical and ethical. As we move towards a future of increasingly automated mobility, it's imperative that the decisions we make are informed, thoughtful and, above all, inclusive. In this way, we can ensure that the benefits of automation and autonomous vehicles are enjoyed by everyone, not just a small elite.

## Traffic Optimization and Fleet Management

Traffic optimization and fleet management are two areas where AI is making a tangible impact, transforming age-old ways of doing things into something dynamic and adaptive. In a world where cities are increasingly congested and the demand for freight transport continues to grow, AI offers innovative solutions that could revolutionize how we move and how we transport goods.

Let's start with traffic optimization. Cities around the world are notoriously congested, with millions of vehicles driving down congested streets every day. This congestion is not only a source of frustration for motorists, it also comes at a significant economic and environmental cost. AI is changing this scenario substantially. AI-powered traffic management systems are now monitoring a myriad of variables ranging from road conditions to driving habits in real-time. More and more cities are implementing smart traffic lights that can dynamically adjust to traffic conditions, rather than following a rigid schedule. These traffic lights use algorithms to analyze traffic flow and optimize green and red light times, thus facilitating a smoother flow of vehicles and reducing waiting times.

Traffic flow analysis goes far beyond intelligent traffic lights. AI systems are able to predict congestion points and suggest alternative routes, not only for motorists but also for urban planners. This ability to anticipate and mitigate traffic problems before they occur can have a profound impact on the quality of life in cities, making urban transport more efficient and sustainable.

Now let's move on to fleet management, another industry experiencing a real transformation thanks to AI. Logistics is one of the most complex and expensive industries, involving the coordination of large numbers of vehicles, itineraries and personnel. Managing fleets of trucks, ships and aircraft is an extremely complicated task that requires optimization on multiple levels. Artificial intelligence is now being used to analyze historical and real-time data to optimize itineraries. This means vehicles can be routed more efficiently, avoiding traffic jams and reducing downtime. At the same time, AI can predict when a vehicle might need maintenance, thus enabling preventive interventions that can reduce costs and improve safety.

In the case of fleets of ships, AI can analyze factors such as weather conditions, ocean currents and other data to suggest optimal routes. This not only speeds up transportation, but can also significantly reduce fuel consumption, with both economic and environmental benefits. For aircraft, AI can be used to optimize everything from flight planning to machine maintenance, making air travel more efficient and sustainable.

So in both traffic optimization and fleet management, artificial intelligence is showing its ability to make our transportation systems smarter, more efficient and ultimately more sustainable. As we continue to make advances in AI technology, we are likely to see further improvements that could fundamentally change the way we view and handle mobility. From the motorist benefiting from smarter traffic lights to the large logistics company that can transport goods more efficiently, the implications are vast and deeply transformative.

As technology continues to evolve, applications of AI in traffic optimization and fleet management will become more and more sophisticated. For example, we could see the implementation of interconnected transportation networks where cars, traffic lights, train stations, and even bicycles share real-time data to create a fully synchronized transportation ecosystem. In such a scenario, autonomous vehicles could communicate with each other to avoid collisions and coordinate traffic flow, while traffic lights could receive data from road and vehicle sensors to adjust the timing of light cycles even more precisely. In this ecosystem, the concept of "traffic" could become an anachronism, replaced by a fluid and optimized flow of mobility.

For commercial fleets, AI could go beyond simple routing and maintenance optimization to tailor logistics to specific cargo needs. For example, AI systems could determine the most efficient way to load and unload cargo, considering factors such as weight, fragility and even the optimum temperature for different types of cargo. Furthermore, real-time monitoring technology could allow fleet managers to react to unexpected events, such as road disruptions or adverse weather conditions, dynamically redesigning travel plans to minimize delays.

Another emerging area is the use of AI for sustainability in transportation. Smart energy management and emissions reduction have become key concerns for cities and businesses. Here, AI can play a key role in creating predictive models that can help fleets reduce fuel consumption, for example by suggesting when to switch to eco-efficient driving modes or when to recharge for electric vehicles . Furthermore, AI technologies could be used for the analysis of large amounts of environmental data, helping to plan routes that minimize environmental impact. However, as we welcome these innovations, it is vital to consider the security and ethical implications. Real-time data collection and analysis presents significant data privacy and security issues. Furthermore, while autonomous vehicles hold the promise of reducing accidents caused by human error, we must also prepare for new types of security risks, including potential vulnerabilities to cyberattacks.

AI has the potential to revolutionize the transport and mobility sector, making it more efficient, safer and more sustainable. From making our roads less congested through traffic optimization, to improving the efficiency and sustainability of vehicle fleet management, the possibilities are immense and ever-changing. With careful consideration of the ethical and safety implications, AI could very well be paving the way for the future of transportation and mobility, a future that may be closer than we think.

Transport safety

In a world where mobility and connectivity are becoming more and more complex, transport safety is of growing importance.
At the same time, technological evolution is profoundly changing the transport landscape. At the heart of this transformation is artificial intelligence (AI), a technology that has the power to make transportation systems not only more efficient, but safer as well. This chapter will explore how AI can help improve safety across different modes of transport: land, air, sea and rail.
In the context of land transport, AI can do a lot to reduce road accidents, which often result from human errors such as distraction, tiredness or lack of awareness of road conditions. Cameras and sensors installed in modern vehicles can collect data in real time, which can then be analyzed by intelligent algorithms. These systems can recognize patterns that indicate a potential hazard, such as heavy braking or lane changing, and can alert the driver or even take control of the vehicle to prevent an accident. This is particularly relevant for commercial vehicles such as trucks, where an accident can have catastrophic consequences.
In the aviation sector, AI can help reduce the risk of plane crashes, which while rare, are often devastating. Autopilot systems are already a standard component in many commercial aircraft, but with AI, these technologies can be taken to a new level. For example, AI algorithms can constantly monitor a wide range of variables, from weather conditions to engine data, to anticipate and prevent potential problems. Air traffic control systems can also benefit from AI to more effectively manage congested airspaces, thus reducing the risk of collisions.

Shipping is another sector where safety is paramount, not only for the protection of human lives but also for the preservation of the environment.

Here, AI can help prevent accidents such as collisions and shipwrecks, through intelligent navigation systems that take into account variables such as sea currents, weather conditions and traffic from other vessels. Similarly, predictive maintenance could prevent mechanical failures that could lead to environmental disasters such as oil spills.

We must not forget the railway sector, where AI can optimize traffic management and infrastructure maintenance. For example, AI can analyze real-time and historical data to predict where and when failures or delays might occur, enabling proactive response that improves safety and efficiency. While AI offers these exciting opportunities to improve transportation safety, it is crucial to also consider the ethical implications and potential risks. For example, large-scale data collection and analysis can raise privacy issues. Furthermore, the growing autonomy of AI-powered transportation systems could open up new vulnerabilities in terms of cyber security.

AI has a crucial role to play in improving transportation safety across a wide range of applications, from real-time monitoring algorithms to advanced navigation systems. However, as we move into a future where AI is increasingly integrated into our transportation systems, it is imperative that we address ethical issues and potential risks as seriously as we embrace the tangible benefits.

A holistic approach that balances innovation and accountability will be key to realizing AI's full potential in creating safer transportation systems for all.

As we move towards greater implementation of AI across transportation domains, it is critical to consider how emerging technologies can be integrated harmoniously with existing systems.

This integration is especially crucial to ensure that security is not compromised during the transition period. For example, as autonomous cars gradually enter the road traffic flow, we need to understand how they will interact with human-driven vehicles. AI can play a role here, simulating various scenarios and helping engineers predict how autonomous and human-driven vehicles will coexist on the roads.

Another key issue is education and training. As AI takes on ever more complex functions, drivers, pilots and other operators will need to be trained to collaborate effectively with these new technologies. Some may fear that AI could completely replace humans in these roles, but a more realistic perspective is that of a partnership where AI can perform tasks that are routine, repetitive or dangerous, leaving humans in charge of the tasks. more complex decisions that require deep intuition and understanding.

AI can also contribute to the safety of public transport, an aspect often overlooked when thinking about technological innovation in the field of transport. AI-powered video surveillance systems can monitor bus and train stations for suspicious behavior, while data analytics can help optimize schedules and reduce overcrowding, thereby reducing the risk of accidents.

Standardization is another important element to consider. With different companies and organizations developing their AI-powered solutions, it is crucial that there is some standardization to ensure that all systems are compatible and most importantly, secure. This is especially true when considering cross-border issues, such as international air traffic control or maritime navigation.

And, of course, there is the vital role of regulation. As with any technological advance, it is essential that innovation is balanced by appropriate regulation that ensures public safety. This can be a particular challenge with AI given how quickly the technology is advancing. However, it is crucial that regulatory authorities are proactive in understanding these new technologies and adapting or creating regulations that maintain high safety standards.

AI has tremendous potential to improve safety across all modes of transportation. However, it is crucial that its implementation is done in a thoughtful manner, taking into consideration not only the potential but also the risks and ethical challenges. The road to a safer future of transportation with AI is full of opportunities, but it's one we need to travel with care, awareness and a serious commitment to doing things right.

## Intermodality and Supply Chain Optimization

Intermodality and supply optimization chain have become buzzwords in the modern world of freight transportation and logistics. The complexity of the global distribution network, characterized by a multitude of transport methods, from ships to planes, trucks and trains, makes it essential to use innovative solutions to effectively manage the flow of goods. Artificial intelligence is becoming a crucial component in making these systems more efficient, responsive and ultimately more sustainable.

Let's start with the warehouse management aspect. In the past, warehouse activity was largely manual, requiring significant human effort to manage inventory, prepare orders, and coordinate shipment.

But with the advent of advanced robotics and AI, warehouses are becoming increasingly automated.

We're not just talking about robotic arms sorting items off shelves; AI can predict demand trends based on historical and current data, allowing warehouse managers to optimize the placement of goods. This reduces the time it takes to pick items for an order, increasing efficiency and reducing costs.

But warehouse efficiency is only one piece of the puzzle. Once goods leave the warehouse, they must be transported, often through a complex network involving multiple methods of transportation. That's where intermodality comes into play. The AI can analyze a wide range of variables in real time, such as traffic conditions, waiting times at ports, and even weather conditions, to determine the most efficient route for each cargo. It can also predict bottlenecks in the distribution network and suggest alternative routes before they become a problem, thereby improving timeliness and reducing costs.

In the context of ports, often described as the 'bottleneck' of the supply global chain , AI offers a number of applications ranging from vessel traffic management to space optimization for containers. In the largest and busiest ports in the world, a minute of crane inactivity or a delay in docking a ship can have a ripple effect throughout the supply chain. chain . AI systems that can precisely coordinate these movements, based on a myriad of real-time data and forecasts, not only improve efficiency but also increase the economic return of port operations.

We cannot forget the aspect of sustainability. As awareness of the environmental impact of logistics and freight transport grows, there is growing pressure to make these systems 'greener'.

Here, AI can have a significant impact, for example by optimizing fuel consumption in various modes of transport.

The data can also be used to plan routes that minimize environmental impact, taking into account not only distance, but also factors such as carbon or carbon emissions associated with each route.

Artificial intelligence is becoming a key player in supply modernization and optimization chains and intermodal transport systems. It offers a suite of tools that not only increase efficiency, reduce costs and improve timeliness, but also have the potential to make these systems more sustainable. With the continued growth of global trade and the urgent need for more sustainable transportation systems, applications of AI in this field are set to expand, bringing innovations that were unimaginable just a few years ago.

As AI continues to permeate transportation and logistics management, there is a growing need for horizontal integration. That is, the need to converge different platforms, transport methods, and databases into a unified system. This approach can make the most of the benefits offered by AI, creating a fully synchronized logistics ecosystem.

Take the example of refrigerated transport, a critical component for the food and pharmaceutical industries. Timeliness is essential, but maintaining a constant temperature is also essential for the quality and safety of the products. IoT sensors can monitor the temperature inside shipping containers and send this data to a centralized AI-powered system. The system can then make real-time decisions on how to optimize the temperature inside the container, communicate with the vehicle to adjust the climate controls and, if problems arise, alert the fleet management team to take corrective action.

Traceability is another key aspect that greatly benefits from the use of AI. RFID packets and GPS provide real-time data on the location of goods, but it is AI that can analyze this data along with other variables to make accurate predictions about delivery times or potential delays. This information can be extremely valuable for customers and for managing expectations, as well as for planning further stages of the supply chain .

No less important is the data analysis for preventive maintenance. Trucks, ships and planes are subjected to wear and tear and inevitably need maintenance. AI can predict when a part is likely to fail or when is the optimal time to perform maintenance, based on data from built-in sensors and historical logs. This not only increases the life of the vehicle but also reduces downtime, which can be costly in terms of money and reputation.

And as can be expected, safety is always the basis of every transport and logistics operation. Here, AI can help identify potentially dangerous behavior through real-time monitoring. For example, it could identify abnormal behavior in the way a truck is handled and flag the problem for further investigation. This goes beyond mere compliance , helping companies establish a proactive safety culture.

Artificial intelligence is radically transforming the landscape of intermodal transportation and supply management chain , making everything from warehouse inventory to traffic flows in global ports more efficient, reliable and secure.

Developments in this field are rapid and continuous, with new possibilities constantly emerging.

Each step forward in this direction not only improves the existing logistics network but also lays the foundations for future developments that could be even more revolutionary.

Just as AI is becoming more sophisticated, so is its application in creating a more integrated and optimized transportation ecosystem.

## Personalization and User Experience

hyperconnected world , user experience has become a key factor in the success or failure of any service or product. In the transport and mobility sector, this maxim is no exception.

Indeed, thanks to the rapid advances in artificial intelligence, there is a revolution taking place in the way transportation providers interact with their customers. Personalization and user experience are no longer terms relegated to the world of marketing or design; they have become essential elements for making transport services more efficient, accessible and above all, user-centred.

Let's start by considering the problem of crowding, a constant challenge for any public transport system, and especially in large cities. At first glance, it would seem that crowding is a problem that only an increase in capacity or a decrease in demand can solve. However, with the use of AI, a more nuanced approach is possible. Algorithms can analyze real-time and historical data on transit usage and predict when and where congestion will occur. This information can then be communicated to users through smartphone applications. Instead of arriving at a subway station and finding it impossible to board, a passenger might receive a notice suggesting they take an alternative route, or even wait a few minutes to avoid crowding. This not only improves the user experience but also optimizes the use of the transport system by better distributing the load between different lines or timetables.

When it comes to delays, another bete noire for commuters, AI also has a lot to offer. The more data the algorithms can analyze, the more accurate they become at predicting problems. Algorithms can do more than simply analyze past lags; they can integrate weather information, monitor traffic conditions in real time, and even detect accidents or other disruptions through news and social media. Once processed, this data can provide highly accurate predictions of travel times, allowing travelers to plan accordingly. For example, if the AI predicts that a train will be delayed due to an imminent mechanical failure or bad weather en route, the application could suggest alternatives before the disruption occurs.

The user experience goes beyond simply preventing inconveniences like crowding and delays. It is also a question of comfort, accessibility and even pleasure in the journey. Here, AI can contribute significantly through data analysis of user preferences. For example, a transportation app might notice that a user frequently travels from point A to point B and might start offering you optimal times, routes, and reservation options automatically with a simple click. Or it might detect that a user prefers window seats and do its best to reserve those seats when they're available.

AI is redefining expectations of what great user experience means in the context of transportation and mobility. The computational power and data analysis capabilities of AI enable a level of personalization and proactivity that was unthinkable just a few years ago.

The implications of this revolution go far beyond mere convenience or solving long-standing problems.

They represent a paradigm shift towards a transportation ecosystem that is truly user-centred, making every journey not only more efficient but also more enjoyable.

As this paradigm shift continues, it is essential to consider the ethical implications of personalization through artificial intelligence. While AI can make travellers' lives easier and better, the use of sensitive data also raises important questions regarding privacy and security. For example, while a transit app might use GPS data to provide more efficient routes, this same information could also be used for less noble purposes if it falls into the wrong hands . So, as developers strive to make applications smarter and more useful, they will also need to pay closer attention to how they protect user data and communicate their privacy policies.

Inclusivity is also a crucial point when it comes to personalizing the user experience. If well designed, AI can help make transportation services more accessible to people with different abilities or needs. For example, an app could predict not only the fastest route, but also the most accessible route for a wheelchair user. Or it could warn in advance if a means of transport is equipped with services for the visually impaired or hearing impaired. In this way, AI can play a crucial role in reducing the barriers that often make it difficult for people with special needs to move.

In addition to accessibility, AI-enhanced personalization can contribute to energy efficiency and sustainability. Imagine a system where data about travel habits is used not only to improve the individual experience, but also to optimize the entire transportation system.

Based on passenger flow patterns, an algorithm could redirect means of transport to areas of higher demand, minimizing empty trips and

hence the fuel consumption. This type of dynamic resource management is not only a saving for service providers, but also a step towards a more sustainable future.

Personalization is also capable of transforming the user experience on long-distance travel. For example, in airline flights, AI systems can analyze passengers' preferences for food, seating and entertainment, making each flight a near-tailored experience. And, as already seen in some airlines' custom entertainment systems, this is just the beginning. With the progressive integration of AI, we could see systems that automatically adjust the lighting and temperature conditions according to the preferences or even the physical and mental well-being of passengers, significantly improving comfort during long-haul journeys.

Artificial intelligence has the potential to revolutionize the user experience in every aspect of the transportation system. Whether it's avoiding crowds and delays, providing a previously unimaginable level of personalization, or making travel more inclusive and sustainable, the possibilities are nearly endless. However, it is imperative that this power is used responsibly. As we move towards an increasingly personalized future, we must pay attention to the ethical and social implications of these technologies, ensuring they improve the lives of all, not just some.

## The Future of AI in the Transportation Sector

The future of the transportation sector looks set to be profoundly impacted by artificial intelligence. It is no longer a question of "if", but of "when" and "how". Already implemented AI applications, from self-driving capabilities to traffic management systems, have
demonstrated potential that goes far beyond incremental improvements. We are talking about a real revolution, which could rewrite the rules on how we move, how we deliver goods and how we design urban and transport infrastructures.

However, with great power comes great responsibility. One of the major challenges of the future will be to ensure that this revolution is as ethical as it is effective. For example, while AI could make transportation more efficient, how do we ensure it doesn't magnify existing inequalities, giving preferential access to those who can afford cutting-edge technologies? Furthermore, the ethical treatment of the data collected to feed these systems will be crucial. The promise of traffic optimization based on real-time data could easily turn into a surveillance nightmare if not handled carefully.

No less important is the question of sustainability. AI systems are extremely powerful, but often require enormous amounts of energy to operate. As we explore ways to make transportation more efficient, we must also consider the environmental impact of data centers and the infrastructure needed to support these advanced technologies. Research is already exploring ways to make algorithms more energy efficient, but much more needs to be done.

Sustainable mobility is another theme that will receive a significant boost from AI. Imagine a city where an AI system coordinates all modes of transportation, from public transport to private vehicles, optimizing routes to reduce carbon emissions. In such an ecosystem, EVs could be directed to fast-charging stations at times of low demand, while transit systems could be adjusted in real-time to match vehicle and foot traffic patterns, reducing unnecessary energy waste.

AI can also play a key role in accelerating the transition to cleaner energy sources in the transportation sector. For example, advanced algorithms can be used to optimize the design and operation of hydrogen-powered vehicles or transport networks powered by renewable energy. AI systems can monitor and analyze huge amounts of data in real time to make accurate predictions of energy consumption, enabling better integration of renewable sources into transportation systems.

But perhaps one of the greatest promises of AI in transportation is its potential to improve safety. With advanced sensing and reaction systems, the vehicles of the future will be not only more efficient, but also significantly safer. AI can help reduce the number of road accidents, many of which are caused by human errors, such as distraction or fatigue. Besides saving lives, this will also have a positive impact on the economic cost associated with road accidents, which is substantial.

AI has the potential to revolutionize the transport sector in ways we can currently only imagine, it is crucial to address a range of ethical, social and environmental issues. Only through a holistic approach that takes these different facets into account can we fully realize the benefits that AI has to offer. By proactively addressing these challenges, we can hope to lead the transport sector into a future that is not only more efficient and convenient, but also more equitable and sustainable.

At the same time, we need to consider the potential impact on the labor market. Increasing automation and the use of AI in transportation could threaten jobs that are currently held by humans.

On the other hand, technological evolution often creates new opportunities and new sectors that did not exist before.

Therefore, a crucial part of our vision for the future of transport will have to include training and retraining programs to help workers adapt to change.

In the field of logistics and supply chain, AI offers tools for more efficient planning and management. Algorithms can analyze complex variables ranging from weather conditions to expected delivery times to optimize routes. This not only reduces costs, but also the environmental impact resulting from ineffective transport. Furthermore, advanced predictive systems can anticipate demand, allowing for more efficient and less costly inventory management. It's also possible that AI could help solve some of the transportation sector's biggest infrastructure challenges. For example, in the context of congested cities and transport routes that are running out of capacity, AI can offer alternative solutions to relieve the strain on existing systems. Think of advanced tracking systems that dynamically redistribute traffic flow to avoid traffic jams, or the use of drones to transport goods in hard-to-reach areas.

Personalization and user experience in transportation are set to be transformed by AI. Virtual assistants could provide real-time information on transport schedules, book tickets and even suggest alternative routes in case of delays. Apps of this type could also be integrated with other useful functions, such as booking taxis or sharing vehicles, making the whole travel experience smoother and more seamless.

In all of this, it's crucial not to underestimate the importance of public engagement and transparency in how these technologies are implemented and used.

Active engagement with citizens can help identify and address the privacy, ethics, and security concerns that inevitably arise when it comes to AI and data at scale.

AI has the potential to be a game changer in the transport sector, offering a range of solutions to problems ranging from energy efficiency to road safety. However, to realize this potential, it is essential that AI implementations are guided by a robust ethical framework and that they consider social and environmental impact. In fact, technology is only a tool; the challenge is to use it in such a way as to build a more sustainable, equitable and humane transport system. In this way, AI will not only be a driving force of the next revolution in transportation, but also a contribution to building a better society.

## Transformation of the Aviation Industry

The aviation industry is witnessing a radical transformation thanks to the incursion of artificial intelligence (AI). This is not just an evolution, but a revolution that changes the way we see and experience air travel. Historically, the aviation industry has always been at the forefront of adopting new technologies.

From the introduction of radars to the computerization of control towers, the goal has always been to improve the efficiency and safety of flights. But AI opens a new chapter, offering solutions that were once thought to be science fiction.

Let's take automation as a starting example. Most commercial aircraft are already able to take off, navigate and land semi-autonomously. However, the new generation of AI offers the prospect of fully autonomous aircraft.

Algorithms can learn from the data collected during each flight, thus allowing systems to become increasingly efficient and safer. Crucially, the aircraft's condition is continuously monitored, allowing for real-time corrections that can prevent accidents or mechanical problems.

But automation is just the tip of the iceberg. AI also offers tremendous opportunities in terms of predictive maintenance. Traditionally, aircraft maintenance has been scheduled around time or usage, which can lead to unnecessary downtime or worse, inadequate maintenance. AI can analyze massive amounts of data from aircraft sensors, identify patterns or anomalies, and then predict when a failure is likely to occur. This not only improves safety but also reduces costs associated with delays and mechanical breakdowns.

In addition to the direct benefits for airlines, AI is also transforming the passenger experience. Applications range from customizing in-flight entertainment to virtual assistants that can answer passengers' questions in real time, improving service quality and customer satisfaction. Imagine a system where AI knows your food or entertainment preferences and automatically applies them whenever you travel with a specific airline.

In the context of airport operations, AI can have a significant impact on efficiency and passenger flow.

For example, facial recognition systems could make traditional security checkpoints redundant, dramatically speeding boarding times and reducing opportunities for human error.

These systems can be integrated with other technologies, such as big data and the Internet of Things ( IoT ), to create a fully synchronized ecosystem that optimizes every aspect of airport operations.

Aviation safety is another sector that will greatly benefit from the adoption of AI. Advanced monitoring and analysis systems can identify potential security threats more accurately and in real time, from bad weather to mechanical failures, and even potential acts of terrorism. AI can be used to simulate millions of different scenarios, providing pilots and ground personnel with valuable data that can be used to make quick and informed decisions in emergency situations. Therefore, it is essential to consider the ethical and social implications of growing automation in the aviation sector. While AI offers the promise of increased efficiency and security, the elimination of human jobs in this area is an issue that requires close scrutiny. A balanced approach that maximizes the benefits of AI while maintaining high ethical and social standards should be adopted.

The incorporation of AI into the aviation industry promises to be transformational. The opportunities to increase efficiency, improve security, and elevate the customer experience are enormous. However, this transition needs to be managed carefully, balancing the promises of technological innovation with ethical and social considerations to realize a future where AI contributes to a safer, more efficient and humane aviation industry.

As the aviation industry immerses itself more and more in the world of artificial intelligence, it becomes imperative to develop governance and regulatory frameworks that keep pace with innovations. Until now, much of aviation regulation has been developed in an era where automation and data analytics were far from as pervasive as they are today.

This regulatory gap presents a challenge, but also an opportunity to rethink how laws and policies can evolve to better serve a changing society.

A particularly thorny issue is that of liability in the event of an accident or breakdown. In the traditional world of aviation, the lines of accountability are pretty clear: there's a human pilot who makes final decisions and can be held accountable for mistakes. But in a system dominated by algorithms, establishing blame becomes more complex. Is the algorithm faulty? Was it a mistake in the training phase of the AI model? Or maybe it was a problem in how the data was collected or interpreted? Answering these questions will be crucial to maintaining a high degree of trust in the system.

Ethics is another element that needs serious reflection. For example, how is passenger data handled? With AI providing the ability to significantly personalize the travel experience, the amount of data collected will increase exponentially. Everything from food preferences to travel habits could be logged and analyzed. While this offers undoubted convenience and personalization benefits, it also raises legitimate privacy and data security concerns. Not to mention the environmental impact. The aviation industry is a major contributor to greenhouse gas emissions, and while AI can help optimize routes and improve fuel efficiency, true sustainability will only be achieved through more profound changes. For example, AI could accelerate the development and adoption of alternative and sustainable fuels, helping airlines make more informed decisions about their use.

The introduction of artificial intelligence in the aviation sector represents one of the most significant industrial transformations of recent times. However, like any revolution, it presents both opportunities and challenges. Airlines, regulators and passengers must work together to ensure the potential of AI is realized in ways that benefit all stakeholders, without compromising safety, ethics or the environment. The road ahead is long and fraught with uncertainty, but with the right combination of innovation and thinking, AI has the power to take the aviation industry to extraordinary new heights.

# Chapter 9: AI in Natural Language Processing:

In recent years, artificial intelligence has quietly invaded many aspects of our daily lives, from the way we move and work, to the way we interact with the world around us. But one of the most intriguing areas where AI is making quiet, yet significant waves, is natural language processing (NLP). While the spotlight is often on autonomous vehicles and robotics, NLP works behind the scenes, driving interactions ranging from simple voice commands on our smartphones to real-time analysis of millions of tweets .

Natural language processing is essentially the ability of machines to understand, interpret, and generate human language in a way that is both useful and meaningful. This may seem simple on the surface, but human language is extraordinarily complex, loaded with nuance, context and unspoken rules that humans unconsciously assimilate from childhood. It's a field that has fascinated computer scientists, linguists, and philosophers for decades, if not centuries. But only in the last few years, thanks to the advent of deep learning and big data, have these machines become sophisticated enough to come close to an authentic interpretation of human language.

The importance of these innovations cannot be emphasized enough. In an increasingly globalized world, the ability to communicate effectively across language and cultural barriers is more valuable than ever. And it's not just a matter of translating from one language to another. NLP offers the promise of more contextualized translations that take into account not only words, but also intrinsic meaning, tone, and sentiment elements that are often lost when we rely on literal translations.

But translation is just the tip of the iceberg. Sentiment analysis, for example, is becoming a powerful tool for companies trying to understand consumer opinion, and it can have applications ranging from marketing to politics. Daily interactions are also changing: virtual assistants are becoming more sophisticated, able to handle an ever wider range of tasks and understand commands given in natural language rather than through specific hard-coded commands .

In this context, it becomes crucial to explore in depth how AI is influencing NLP, and how this interaction is, in turn, shaping numerous aspects of our society. The aim of this chapter is therefore to provide a deep dive into this fascinating topic, examining various aspects such as machine translation, sentiment analysis, the use of chatbots and virtual assistants, and applications in education and communication. However, as with any emerging technology, AI-powered NLP is not without its challenges and ethical issues. From the risk of biases built into algorithms to the implication of job loss due to automation, having a balanced view of the field is critical. With this chapter, we hope to offer a comprehensive overview that not only highlights the potential of NLP to improve communication and access to information, but also highlights the complexities and responsibilities that these potentials entail.

So as we continue in this exploration, let's keep in mind not only the technical capabilities that AI is bringing to NLP, but also the broader social, ethical, and even philosophical implications of this fusion of machine and language. In a world where the written and spoken word is so powerful, understanding the potential and limitations of NLP may not only be interesting from an academic point of view, but also fundamental for the future of our social and global coexistence.

# Machine Translation and Sentiment Analysis: A Smaller, But More Complex World

In a world shrinking due to globalization and interconnectedness, the language barrier remains one of the most persistent obstacles to understanding and collaboration. Traditionally, overcoming this obstacle has required the mediation of human translators and interpreters, professionals capable of understanding not only grammar and vocabulary, but also the subtle cultural and contextual nuances that can change the meaning of a sentence. But with the advent of AI-powered machine translation, these dynamics are rapidly changing.

Today's machine translation algorithms are significantly more advanced than those of previous generations. Using techniques such as deep learning and neural networks, these systems are able to "learn" from the context, making translations increasingly precise and natural. But it's context analysis that really sets modern machine translation systems apart. Instead of focusing on a word-by-word translation, today's algorithms consider the entire sentence or even the paragraph, allowing for a translation that takes into account the general meaning rather than specific details.

This level of sophistication has opened up new opportunities in business, diplomacy and education. For example, a company with offices in several countries can now communicate more effectively with its employees and customers without the need for interpreters. Furthermore, machine translation tools are becoming more and more integrated into social media platforms, allowing for a wider dissemination of news and information.

Imagine a newspaper article written in Japanese that is automatically translated into English, Spanish, French and dozens of other languages, making the information accessible to a global audience almost instantly.

As impressive as it is, machine translation isn't the only area where natural language processing is making significant progress. Another fundamental area is the analysis of feelings. In an age where huge amounts of data are generated every day, the ability to analyze and interpret this data has become vital. And when it comes to unstructured data like text—think social media comments, product reviews, or interviews—sentiment analysis offers an invaluable tool for understanding public opinion.

Sentiment analysis uses NLP algorithms to identify and categorize the opinions expressed in a piece of text, in order to determine the author's attitude towards a particular topic or product. This can range from simple positive or negative evaluations to more complex analyzes that consider emotions such as happiness, sadness, anger or surprise. Companies of all types are using sentiment analytics to improve their products and services. If a new product receives negative reviews, sentiment analytics can help identify specific issues that may not be apparent through traditional analytics methods.

But the applications go beyond the business world. For example, during elections, sentiment analysis can

provide valuable insights into public opinion far beyond what can be obtained through polling. Similarly, in healthcare, understanding sentiment can be used to identify early signs of conditions such as depression or anxiety, often manifested through changes in speech and tone.

In both of these domains — machine translation and sentiment analysis — AI is providing tools that not only improve efficiency, but also have the potential to create deeper, more human understanding. And as the technology continues to improve, we're likely to see even more innovative and impactful applications.

However, as with every technological advance, new ethical dilemmas and challenges also emerge. For example, while machine translation can serve as a bridge between cultures, it can also be a medium for spreading misinformation or bias. Similarly, sentiment analysis can be used to manipulate public opinion or to invade privacy. These ethical issues represent a gray area that society has yet to fully address. While algorithms can provide a translation or analysis of feelings with a level of precision never seen before, blind trust in these systems can lead to errors in judgment or a distorted understanding of reality.

The issue of liability is another aspect that deserves attention. For example, who is responsible if a translation algorithm provides an incorrect translation that leads to a serious diplomatic or medical misunderstanding? Or, how do we handle the large-scale emotional data collection that sentiment analysis might involve?

These questions require serious thought and possibly legal regulation to ensure that the technology is used ethically and responsibly.

Furthermore, there is the problem of data quality. AI algorithms are only as good as the data they are trained on.

If that data is biased or incomplete, the algorithms will produce unreliable results. This is especially true in sentiment analysis, where cultural and contextual nuances can have a significant impact on meaning. Linguistic diversity, with dialects, jargon and colloquialisms, presents an additional challenge for forming accurate algorithms.

It is clear that machine translation and sentiment analysis are already having a profound impact on how we interact with the world and with information.

The scale of this impact will only extend as we refine our algorithms and integrate these tools deeper into our reporting and analytics systems.

In any case, as we approach a future in which linguistic and interpretative barriers become less and less obstacles to communication and understanding, we must also face the ethical and practical challenges that emerge from this new frontier.

In summary, AI in machine translation and sentiment analytics offers incredible opportunities for a more connected and informed world, it also presents its own set of challenges ranging from data and training quality to ethics and accountability. As a society, it is imperative that we address these issues proactively, ensuring that technological innovation is balanced by human and moral considerations. As we move forward into an increasingly interconnected world, machine translation and sentiment analytics will serve as indispensable tools for interpreting and understanding the growing amount of data being generated every day. But as with any powerful tool, the key will be how we use it, and for what purpose. With the right combination of technological innovation and ethical awareness, the potential for a more understood and empathetic world is within reach.

## Chatbots and Virtual Assistants

In the digital age, the way people interact with technology and access information is undergoing a profound change. Virtual assistants and chatbots , often powered by natural language processing (NLP) algorithms, are reshaping human-machine interaction in ways that were unthinkable just a decade ago. These artificial agents, integrated into websites, applications or smart devices, are transforming a wide range of industries, from customer service to marketing, from healthcare to education.

A virtual assistant, like Apple's Siri or Amazon's Alexa , is now a family member in millions of homes, helping people do things like set alarms, order food, or check the weather forecast with simple voice commands.

These assistants are able to interpret natural language, thanks to sophisticated AI algorithms that use machine learning to adapt and improve with use. As these technologies continue to evolve, their capabilities are becoming more advanced, encompassing not only verbal queries , but also the context in which they are made, allowing for a more natural and useful conversation with the user.

This functionality also extends to enterprise chatbots , which are often the first point of contact between an organization and its customers or users. Modern chatbots aren't just capable of answering frequently asked questions or guiding users through complicated processes ; they are becoming increasingly "intelligent", capable of handling complex requests, escalating problems to human personnel when necessary, and providing personalized responses based on user behavior and preferences. The magic behind these features is a combination of NLP, data analytics, and machine learning, which together allow these systems to deliver an increasingly sophisticated user experience.

But what does all this mean for the future of our way of interacting with machines and with organizations? One of the most obvious implications is that as these virtual assistants and chatbots become more advanced, the barriers to accessing information and services continue to decrease. People with disabilities, for example, can benefit enormously from using voice assistants for tasks they might otherwise find difficult or impossible to perform.

Furthermore, the use of chatbots in healthcare is already enabling more effective patient monitoring and easier access to medical information, helping to bridge the gap between healthcare services and those who need them.

However, as with machine translation and sentiment analytics, the use of chatbots and virtual assistants raises a number of ethical and practical issues that need to be carefully considered.

Privacy is perhaps the most immediate concern. Virtual assistants often have access to a large amount of personal data, from shopping behaviors to health information. How this data is used and who has access to it are questions that require clear and transparent answers from the providers of these services.

Another issue is that of technological dependence. As we rely more and more on these assistants for a variety of functions, there is a risk that we will become less able to perform tasks without their help. This is a topic of debate among experts: while some see the possibility of "tech-assisted stupidity," others argue that virtual assistants and chatbots can actually free us from mundane tasks, allowing us to focus on more creative and rewarding pursuits.

Debating these ethical and social issues is therefore a key part of understanding the growing role of chatbots and virtual assistants in our lives. However, there is no doubt that artificial intelligence is making these interactions more effective and, in many cases, more humane.

For example, some mental health virtual assistants have been developed to provide an initial level of psychological support. They are not a substitute for a trained medical professional, but they can provide a useful "front line" of support for those in need of help. Even in this sensitive application, NLP and AI play a crucial role in setting the emotional tone and providing responses that are appropriate and constructive.

Applications in education represent another fertile ground for the development of chatbots and virtual assistants. Automated tutoring systems can help students overcome difficulties in specific subjects by offering personalized exercises and tracking their progress over time. Teachers, in turn, can use these platforms to gain valuable insights into the strengths and weaknesses of the classroom, allowing them to tailor the curriculum accordingly.

In this way, technology not only enhances the effectiveness of instruction but also provides a way to personalize the learning experience for each student.

These near-futuristic possibilities are exciting, but it's crucial not to lose sight of the current limitations of technology. As advanced as chatbots and virtual assistants may be, they are still a long way from having the contextual understanding and emotional depth that characterize human interactions. Mistakes can happen and, in contexts such as healthcare or emergency situations, the implications can be serious. However, the goal is not to replace human judgment but to enhance it, by providing tools that can handle repetitive tasks or large-scale data, leaving humans free to focus on aspects that require empathy, insight and deep understanding.

The use of chatbots and virtual assistants is radically transforming the nature of human-machine interactions and the relationships between organizations and users.

Driven by the rapid evolution of NLP and other AI technologies, these systems are becoming ever more sophisticated, capable of handling an ever-widening range of tasks and adapting to the individual needs of users. However, with great power also comes great responsibility: as we embark on this new age of digital interaction, we must pay attention to the complex ethical and social issues that arise. Only then can we fully realize the promises of this groundbreaking convergence of artificial intelligence and human language.

## Applications in education and communication

While chatbots and virtual assistants have begun to transform industries like customer service and healthcare, it is in education and communications that we see perhaps some of the most innovative and disruptive applications.

From platforms that support remote learning to systems that facilitate educational engagement, Artificial Intelligence in Natural Language Processing (NLP) is making dramatic changes to how information is transmitted and received.

Take, for example, the use of AI in improving language skills. NLP-based systems are now capable of assessing an individual's level of language proficiency and providing personalized lessons and exercises. Such platforms not only identify grammatical or syntactic errors, but can also understand the complexity of human language to a degree that offers contextual corrections. This not only improves the quality of learning but also makes it more accessible, providing a valuable resource for anyone looking to learn a new language without access to a qualified teacher.

Personalization is a keyword when it comes to AI-powered educational applications. In addition to language learning, educational platforms can use data analytics and machine learning algorithms to understand each student's strengths and weaknesses.

This allows for a more focused approach to learning, where the curriculum is tailored to individual needs. In this way, AI becomes a powerful tool to narrow the gap between students learning at different rates, giving everyone the opportunity to progress effectively.

This principle of personalization can also extend to more advanced levels of education. Imagine a college class where a virtual assistant is able to provide supplemental reading materials or exercises based on each student's performance in previous classes. Instead of a "one size fits all" approach, where all students receive the same type of education, we are faced with a system that adapts and changes based on student needs and performance. Not only could this improve academic outcomes, but it could also provide a more challenging and engaging context for learning.

The impact of NLP technology on education and communication is not limited only to formal learning contexts. Organizations such as museums, art galleries and science centers are starting to use chatbots and virtual assistants to enhance the visitor experience. A virtual assistant could, for example, provide detailed information about a work of art or historical artifact, answering questions in real time and offering context that might otherwise be missed. In this way, AI can serve as a sort of 'digital curator', enriching cultural and educational experience without replacing the importance of human interaction.

In the field of communication, AI and NLP are making great strides in improving accessibility. For people with disabilities, for example, NLP-based technologies are making it easier to communicate and access information.

Advanced speech recognition software can turn speech into text and vice versa, while translating solutions
in real time they can overcome language barriers like never before. The implications of these innovations are immense, ranging from facilitating more inclusive interactions to providing new tools for individual and collective empowerment.

But as with any emerging technology, there are challenges ahead. Issues related to data privacy, security and ethics remain at the heart of public debate. Furthermore, while AI can personalize education, there is also the risk of creating learning 'bubbles', where students are only exposed to information and perspectives that reinforce their pre-existing beliefs. These are complex issues that require deep and thoughtful discussion by educators, developers and policy makers.

Applications of AI in Natural Language Processing are radically transforming the landscape of education and communication.

From providing personalized and accessible learning to enhancing inclusiveness and engagement, these technologies represent a new frontier in the evolution of education and society. However, it is crucial that these innovations are guided by careful consideration of their ethical and social implications. Only then can we harness the full potential of AI to create a more equal, inclusive and educated future. When you think about the road traveled in just a few years, it's hard not to be optimistic about the future of applications of AI in Natural Language Processing in the fields of education and communication. The coming years could see the emergence of even more intelligent and intuitive systems, capable of performing ever more sophisticated pedagogical functions. Yet, as always, with great potential comes great responsibility. AI offers the opportunity to revolutionize the way we think about education, shifting the emphasis from merely transferring information to creating learning environments.

learning that is flexible, personalized and, above all, student-centred. But at this point new questions emerge: in a world increasingly dependent on technology, what skills will be considered essential for the citizens of the future? And how can we ensure that these advanced pedagogical tools are accessible to all, regardless of their socio-economic background?

The answers to these questions could shape the future not just of education, but of society as a whole. We could see the birth of a generation of individuals who are not only better educated, but also more adept at critical thinking, problem solving and adaptability – all essential skills in a rapidly changing world. But for that to happen, it is essential that AI in education is implemented ethically and responsibly.

Similarly, in the field of communication, we must be aware of the potential of AI to create not only opportunities but also inequalities. The ability to personalize information can be a double-edged sword.

On the one hand, it offers the possibility of providing more relevant and useful content for each individual. On the other hand, it runs the risk of creating echo chambers in which people are only exposed to viewpoints that reinforce their pre-existing beliefs and prejudices. And then there is the matter of disinformation. With the advent of increasingly sophisticated text-to-speech and text-generation technologies, the potential for the creation of " fake news" or deceptive content is increasing. Educating people on how to discern reliable from unreliable information becomes increasingly important. The same technologies that could be used to deceive can also be used to educate, but this requires a holistic approach that goes beyond simple technology implementation.

As AI has the potential to revolutionize education and communication, true success will be determined by the human – by the ways we choose to use these powerful new technologies and the ethical standards we set to guide them. If used wisely, Artificial Intelligence technologies in the field of Natural Language Processing can improve both individual and collective life, opening new paths for personal development and societal progress. But as with any powerful tool, the secret lies in responsible and conscious use. And in this, as in so many other aspects of life, education and communication will be key.

# Chapter 10: Chapter 10: Future of AI: Opportunities and Challenges

The twenty-first century will undoubtedly be marked by the emergence and maturation of artificial intelligence, a technology that not only promises to revolutionize the way industries, economies and institutions operate, but also the fundamental structures of societies and their interactions. When it comes to discussing the future of artificial intelligence, or AI, we're in territory fraught with expectations, some realistic, some speculative, and still others bordering on science fiction. But whichever angle you approach it from, it's impossible to ignore the incalculable impact this technology will have on the fabric of our world.

As AI begins to permeate every aspect of our daily lives, from street navigation to online shopping advice, from healthcare services to energy management, it has become urgent not only to understand its scope but also to responsibly shape its evolutionary path . The drive towards digitization and automation, of which AI is a crucial component, represents an epochal turning point which, if directed wisely, has the potential to lead to extraordinary advances in the quality of human life. But it is precisely this potential that makes a critical analysis of the challenges it poses indispensable. For example, AI has already begun to show its effectiveness in accelerating medical research. Using sophisticated algorithms to analyze large datasets has made it possible to identify correlations and patterns that would otherwise have remained hidden from the human eye.

This has significant implications for the early diagnosis and treatment of disease, not to mention long-term implications for the personalization of medicine.

Similarly, the computational power of AI has been exploited to optimize logistics in numerous industrial sectors, improving efficiency and reducing costs.

However, alongside these positive developments, worrying problems and issues are also emerging. AI is not just a force for good; it also represents a series of risks and uncertainties ranging from ethical implications to information security, from technological unemployment to the aggravation of inequalities. Its role in strengthening or weakening democratic structures is still the subject of much debate, as is its impact on global geopolitical dynamics.

Faced with this complex scenario, this chapter aims to provide a detailed and in-depth analysis of the opportunities and challenges posed by the advance of AI. The aim is to go beyond the hypothetical and sensational to explore future scenarios grounded in data and facts, considering both the social and economic impact and the crucial role humanity must play in shaping this future. Through this exam, we will embark on a journey that will take us from the frontiers of technological innovation to the frontiers of ethics and philosophy, seeking to understand how AI can be guided in a way that serves the best interests of humanity as a whole .

Exploring future scenarios: Social and economic impact

One of the most intriguing but also most worrying aspects of artificial intelligence is its potential to disrupt existing social and economic structures. Take, for example, automation. While AI-driven automation can lead to more efficient production and more rational use of resources, it can also lead to mass unemployment in certain job categories. Some jobs are easier to automate than others, and people in these sectors will be the first to face the problem of outplacement.

It is not only a matter of job losses, but also of the quality of the jobs that are created to replace those lost. AI is often better suited to repetitive, rote jobs, which could lead to a polarization of the labor market, with a growing number of high-skill and low-skill jobs, while in-between positions disappear. In such a scenario, we are called to consider how to restructure our economies and our education systems to prepare people to face this new world.

Beyond automation, we need to consider the impact of AI on privacy and surveillance. While AI techniques such as facial recognition and data analytics are becoming more advanced, so is their application in mass surveillance systems and individual behavior monitoring. The key question here is not just whether these technologies should be used, but how they can be regulated to prevent abuse by authorities or corporations.

Another area where AI is showing a significant impact is healthcare. With the help of sophisticated algorithms, it is possible not only to improve the diagnosis and treatment of diseases, but also to tailor treatment plans to suit individual patient needs. AI can also play a key role in healthcare resource management, helping to optimize the allocation of doctors, nurses and equipment during periods of high demand.

These are just a few of the many areas where AI has the potential to revolutionize the way we live. But each of these changes brings with it a set of challenges that we must be prepared to face.

While AI can make systems more efficient, it can also introduce new types of vulnerabilities. For example, an AI-based medical diagnosis system could be prone to errors or manipulations that could have serious consequences for patients.

And while AI can optimize the use of resources, it could also be used to reinforce existing inequalities, concentrating resources and opportunities in the hands of the few at the expense of the many.

The question, therefore, is not whether AI will impact society and the economy; this impact is now inevitable. The real question is how we can steer this impact to be as beneficial as possible while avoiding the pitfalls and dangers that this new technology undoubtedly presents.

To do this, it is essential to directly address the opportunities and challenges that AI poses, which forms the heart of the next segment of this chapter.

## Insight into opportunities and challenges

The opportunities offered by artificial intelligence are tremendous, but these opportunities are not without obstacles. As we have seen, automation could eliminate certain types of work, but it could also pave the way for new professions and new ways of doing business that we currently cannot even imagine. The key point here is the need for a balanced and thoughtful approach that takes into account both the inherent potential and limitations of using AI.

In the healthcare sector, for example, algorithms could provide faster and more accurate diagnoses, speeding up the treatment process and reducing the pressure on healthcare professionals. But this raises important ethical questions: what are the criteria for deciding whether an algorithm is "precise" enough to be used in clinical settings? And how do we ensure that the data on which these algorithms are trained is representative of all demographic groups, avoiding implicit biases that could harm already disadvantaged communities?

The opportunities in surveillance and security are also doubled.

On the one hand, AI can provide more effective ways to prevent crimes and ensure safety. On the other hand, the same power can be used to invade privacy and limit personal freedoms if not properly regulated. This is particularly true in authoritarian political regimes, but also in democracies, where the temptation to "facilitate" the work of security agencies could lead to an erosion of civil liberties.

AI has the power to decentralize access to information and knowledge. AI-powered online learning platforms, for example, could make high-quality education available to anyone with an internet connection. But, even then, there is a risk that such platforms could be used to propagate disinformation or bias, either intentionally or due to limitations in how the algorithms are programmed.

In this complex panorama of opportunities and challenges, the question that arises is: how to balance these opposing elements? This is where humanity's role in driving the evolution of AI comes into play, a theme that will form the concluding part of this chapter. The responsible management of the potential of AI requires a multidisciplinary collaboration between technologists, ethicists , legislators and, ultimately, the whole social fabric. Only through open and honest dialogue about these issues can we hope to guide the development of AI in a way that maximizes benefits and minimizes risks. And to do that, we need to consider what our role is, as a society and as individuals, in shaping the future of artificial intelligence.

## Humanity's role in driving the evolution of AI

The design, implementation and regulation of artificial intelligence is ultimately a reflection of human values. If we want AI to be a tool for the collective good, we need to be actively involved in it

determine the ethical and moral principles that guide it.

This is a difficult but much-needed task that requires the participation of all stakeholders, from the scientific community to policy-makers, from business leaders to the general public.

Take, for example, the case of autonomous vehicles. When programmed correctly, these vehicles have the potential to dramatically reduce traffic accidents caused by human error.

But this raises a number of ethical questions. How should an autonomous vehicle be programmed to react in an emergency situation where all options carry some level of risk to human life? The answer to this question is not only technical, but profoundly ethical and should be the result of a broad public debate.

Another crucial aspect is transparency. Many of the most advanced AI technologies, such as deep neural networks, are often described as "black boxes" that perform calculations that humans don't understand. If we are to entrust critical decisions to these systems, it's imperative that we understand how they work, or at least that we have ways to interrogate them about the decisions they make. This is especially true in areas such as forensics or healthcare, where decisions can have direct and significant implications for people's lives.

Governance of AI is another critical issue that requires collective action. As AI makes its way into more and more aspects of our lives, the need for a regulatory framework becomes ever more pressing. Who should be responsible when an algorithm makes a bad decision? How can we ensure that AI is used ethically and responsibly? These are questions that cannot be left to tech companies or governments alone, but require a robust governance structure involving all major societal players.

The last point to consider concerns the aspect of inclusiveness . AI, like any other technology, is not immune to social biases that can be embedded in the data it is trained on. From medical diagnosis to legal decisions, from facial recognition to personnel selection, it is crucial to ensure that AI does not perpetuate existing social inequalities but instead helps to mitigate them.

AI holds both enormous promise and a complex set of challenges. To successfully navigate these uncertain waters, a holistic approach is needed that puts humanity at the heart of AI evolution.

We need to be proactive in shaping the ethical, social and political landscape in which AI is meant to operate. Only through joint efforts can we ensure that AI is developed and used in a way that the benefits vastly outweigh the risks, leading humanity towards a safer, more equitable and prosperous future.

# Conclusions: AI as a Bridge between the Present and the Future

As we prepare to conclude this journey through the universe of artificial intelligence, it is essential to put into perspective the context within which all this occurs. Artificial intelligence has become one of the most powerful and transformative forces of our time, ranging from invisible algorithms that regulate the details of our daily lives, to frontier research that opens up new possibilities in science and medicine. But unlike many other technologies, AI possesses a unique power of self-reflection: it invites us to question who we are, what it means to be intelligent, and ultimately what role we want technology to play in shaping the contours of our lives. future.

Artificial intelligence, in this sense, is not just a set of advanced technological tools. It is a lens through which to examine fundamental questions relating to ethics, society, education and human evolution. It is a bridge, a connection between the present we live in and the future that awaits us. How solid this bridge is, however, depends on how we address the various challenges and opportunities that emerge from this ongoing revolution. If built wisely, this bridge can lead us to a future of prosperity, equity and well-being. But if the foundations are weak, if we ignore the ethical dilemmas and social implications, we risk erecting an unstable passage that could collapse under the weight of its own contradictions. For this reason, this chapter of the book is both a reflection and a synthesis. Here, we bring together the various threads of discussion we've woven in previous chapters to create a more complete picture of the AI landscape.

From its role in shaping industry and healthcare to its ability to transform language and communication, we address the many ways AI impacts our lives.

And as we look to the future, maintaining a sense of balance and perspective is essential. AI is a powerful force, but it is also a man-made tool. Its effects, both positive and negative, are the result of the choices we make today. In this concluding chapter, we strive to provide a balanced and thoughtful view of what might come, to examine the exciting opportunities as well as the troubling challenges, and to contemplate the crucial role each of us can play in leading this revolutionary technological adventure.

Ultimately, the story of artificial intelligence is also the story of humanity — a narrative that is still being written. We conclude, therefore, not with a full stop, but with a suspension point, leaving the door open to the infinite possibilities that the future has to offer. And what this future becomes will, to a large extent, depend on how we choose to cross the bridge between the present and what is to come.

If there is one fundamental message we hope to have conveyed in this book, it is that artificial intelligence is as much a product of our ingenuity as it is an actor that will profoundly affect our future. It is not an omnipotent and independent force, but rather a mirror reflecting both our highest ideals and our most manifest contradictions. In this sense, AI is not just a technological challenge; it is an ethical, social and ultimately human challenge.

T he technology continues to evolve, we must never lose sight of the fact that it is human beings who program the algorithms and define the success criteria. We decide which problems to address and how to address them. And while AI can perform calculations at a speed and with an accuracy that far exceeds our capabilities, it is incapable of exercising moral judgment, perceiving beauty, or experiencing love and compassion. These remain uniquely human domains, and it is these traits that we must value and protect as we navigate the age of artificial intelligence.

If we are to seize the opportunities offered by AI — from personalized medicine to sustainable mobility, from inclusive education to participatory democracy — we must also be proactive in mitigating the risks. We must address questions of privacy, ethics and justice with the same urgency and commitment with which we pursue technological innovations. Similarly, we must be vigilant in ensuring that the benefits of AI are distributed fairly, so that everyone, not just a small elite, can enjoy the fruits of progress.

This requires collective awareness and shared commitment. It involves the participation not only of engineers and scientists, but also of philosophers, artists, legislators, educators and, indeed, all members of society. Each of us has a role to play in shaping the future of artificial intelligence, and therefore the future of humanity. And as we approach the horizon of this uncharted future, the invitation is to take this responsibility seriously, with humility, but also with a sense of hope and wonder.

Therefore, as we close this book, let us not consider it a conclusion, but rather a beginning. The story of AI is still being written, and the blank pages that follow are an open invitation: an invitation to think, to discuss, to experiment and, above all, to act. Together, we have the opportunity, and perhaps even the duty, to shape a technology that can amplify the best of what it means to be human, building a future that we can not only imagine, but are proud to pass on to future generations.

In the race towards innovation, ethics and awareness are not optional, but essential imperatives. AI is more than a set of algorithms; it is a lens through which we see ourselves and the world around us. It can magnify our noblest aspirations, but also reflect our subtlest biases.

The responsibility for navigating this double potential rests with each of us. We cannot allow technology to be an excuse for ethical indifference or disregard for basic human principles.

From equitable access to medical treatments to safeguarding individual privacy, from sustainable mobility decisions to justice in the distribution of resources, our ethical conduct in these matters will define not only the future of AI, but also the moral fabric of the society we are in. building. Every choice we make along this path will shape our collective destiny. Therefore, the invitation is clear: let's face the adventure of artificial intelligence with one eye open to extraordinary innovation and the other fixed on the values that make human life extraordinary.

We act with awareness, we act ethically, and above all, we act together.

Because it is only through the union of technology and humanity that we will realize a future in which both can thrive.

# Artificial intelligence

1. OpenAI GPT-3: One of the largest neural networks for text generation, used in a variety of applications ranging from creative writing to customer support.

2. DeepMind's AlphaGo and AlphaFold : AlphaGo is known for defeating the world champion in Go, while AlphaFold made groundbreaking advances in protein structure prediction.

3. Waymo : A subsidiary of Alphabet Inc . (the parent company of Google) which is developing technology for autonomous vehicles.

4. Tesla Autopilot : While not fully autonomous, Tesla's driver assistance system is one of the most advanced commercially available.

5. IBM Watson: Used in various industries such as healthcare and customer service for data analysis and natural language interpretation.

6. Nvidia DLSS: Deep Learning Super Sampling is an artificial intelligence technology that improves graphics in video games.

7. Boston Dynamics' Spot: A quadrupedal robot that can navigate harsh environments and is used in various industries, from industry to scientific research.

8. BERT ( Bidirectional Encoder Representations from Transformers ): A natural language model that has

shown remarkable results in a variety of language processing tasks.

9. Salesforce Einstein: An artificial intelligence suite that provides insights and data analysis to improve customer relationship management.

10. Advanced Chatbots like Mitsuku and Replika : These chatbots use advanced natural language processing techniques to deliver more natural and lifelike conversations.

# Artificial Intelligence for everyone

1. **Google Assistant and Apple's Siri** : Virtual assistants on mobile devices that can help with tasks like web research, setting reminders, and answering basic questions.

2. **Amazon Alexa** : A virtual assistant featured in Amazon's Echo smart speakers , with a wide variety of " skills " or applications that can be activated.

3. **Chatbot like Replika** : A chatbot with which you can conduct conversations on a wide range of topics.

4. **OpenAI's GPT-2** : While the larger GPT-3 version is generally only accessible via API and often has an associated cost, smaller models like GPT-2 have been released for public use and are available for training and development. edit.

5. **TensorFlow and PyTorch** : While not AIs per se, these open-source libraries allow users to build and train their own AI models.

6. **Zapier** : A service that allows you to automate workflows between different web applications, using a form of artificial intelligence to identify and create " Zaps " or automated actions.

7. **Wit.ai** : A platform for building natural language applications that can be integrated into other applications or services.

8. **hugging Face's Transformers Library** : A library for working with templates like BERT and GPT-2. It is research oriented but is accessible enough for developers.

9. **Quillbot** : An AI-powered rewriting and paraphrasing tool that is free and easy to use.

10. **Otter.ai** : A transcription service that uses AI to convert voice conversation into text.

11. **DeepArt** : A tool that uses neural networks to transform your photos into works of art based on the styles of famous painters.

12. **Quick , Draw !** : An online game from Google that uses machine learning to guess what you're drawing in real time.

13. **FaceApp** : An app that uses AI to edit photos of faces, adding smiles, aging people, changing gender, etc.

14. **Grammarly** : A writing assistant that uses AI to fix grammatical errors, improve style, and even suggest an appropriate tone.

15. **Rasa** : An open source AI that allows users to build conversational chatbots . It is versatile enough to be used in different messaging applications.

16. **Pandorabots** : A platform to build and implement AIML ( Artificial Intelligence Markup Language) based chatbots .

17. **DataRobot** : A self-learning tool that helps companies build predictive models without necessarily being data science experts.

18. **Mailchimp** : Primarily known as an email marketing tool, Mailchimp also offers AI-powered features like sending time optimization.

19. **MonkeyLearn** : An AI-powered text analysis tool that can extract information, tag texts, and much more.

20. **Blippar** : An augmented reality app that uses AI to identify objects in the real world through your mobile device's camera.

21. **Zapier** : While not strictly an AI app , Zapier uses intelligent algorithms to help you automate workflows between different web applications.

22. **Dialogflow** : A platform from Google to build chatbots and voice assistants that can be integrated into a variety of applications, from websites to mobile apps .

23. **Wit.ai** : Similar to Dialogflow , it allows you to build speech and text applications that can understand natural language.

24. **Prisma** : An app that uses neural networks to turn photos into images that look like famous painting techniques.

25. **Gboard** : Google's keyboard uses AI to suggest text completion and improve word prediction as you type.

26. **Quillbot** : An online paraphraser that uses AI to help users rephrase or synthesize texts.

27. **Otter.ai** : A service that offers real-time audio transcriptions, using AI to recognize spoken language.

28. **Loomie** : An app that creates custom 3D avatars using artificial intelligence to map facial expressions.

29. **Drift** : A marketing and sales chatbot platform that uses AI to automate customer interactions.

30. **Freenome** : Although not a general public application, Freenome uses AI to diagnose cancer early through blood tests.

31. **Grammarly** : A browser extension and desktop application that uses AI to improve your writing, correct grammar errors, and suggest better styles and tones.

32. **Replika** : A chatbot designed to converse like a human, with the aim of acting as a "virtual friend" to the user.

33. **Kuki** : A cross-platform chatbot that is used for various purposes from customer support to lead capture .

34. **Blippar** : An app that uses augmented reality and artificial intelligence to provide information about objects and places through your smartphone's camera.

35. **AIVA** : A music composition engine that uses AI to create music tracks for different genres and styles.

36. **SoundHound** : A music recognition app that uses AI to identify songs and also to give voice commands like a virtual assistant.

37. **OpenAI's GPT-3** : While not directly accessible to the general public, various services use this powerful language generation technology for a variety of applications, from creative writing to natural language processing.

38. **Pandorabots** : A platform that allows you to build and host chatbots with learning capabilities.

39. **CureMetrix** : While focused on the healthcare sector, this platform uses AI to improve the accuracy of mammograms.

40. **Citymapper** : An urban navigation app that uses AI to provide optimized routes using different modes of public transport.

41. **Quillbot** : An AI-powered paraphrasing tool that helps rephrase sentences or paragraphs, popular among writing students and professionals.

42. **TrueLayer** : An interface that uses AI to allow access and management of financial data, optimizing banking and financial services.

43. **Zapier** : While it's not solely AI-powered, it uses intelligent algorithms to automate tasks across different web applications.

44. **Nutonomy** : A company dedicated to creating autonomous vehicles for public transport, improving transport efficiency and reducing accidents.

45. **Jasper AI** : A text generator that uses AI to create written content for purposes such as marketing, blogosphere and academic writing.

46. **Deep 6 AI** : A tool that accelerates patient recruitment for clinical trials, using machine learning to find suitable candidates faster.

47. **H20.ai** : A platform that offers a set of tools for data analysis, machine learning and AI modeling, focusing on accessibility for non-experts.

48. **SenseTime** : Specializing in visual and facial recognition, this company uses AI in security and surveillance applications.

49. **Rainbird** : An automated reasoning system that helps companies make more informed decisions by simulating the human decision-making process.

www.ingramcontent.com/pod-product-compliance
Lightning Source LLC
La Vergne TN
LVHW051322050326
832903LV00031B/3318